From Puzzles to Projects

From Puzzles to Projects: Solving Problems all the Way

John and Ann Baker

HEINEMANN
Portsmouth, NH

HEINEMANN EDUCATIONAL BOOKS, INC.
361 Hanover Street, Portsmouth, NH 03801-3959
Offices and agents throughout the world

First published in the USA in 1993 by Heinemann

First published in 1986 in Australia by
Thomas Nelson Australia
102 Dodds Street
South Melbourne 3205

ISBN 0 435 08337 6

Cover photograph by Rudi Everts
Typeset in Italia Medium by Dovatype
Printed in Hong Kong

CONTENTS

PREFACE

This book was developed during a three year research period. In that time we were able to visit schools in Leicestershire, Nottinghamshire, London, Devonshire, Sussex and Buckinghamshire. We would have been unable to carry out this work without the help of Maurice Edwards, Hugh Burkhardt, Hugh Neil and Margaret Brown, Libby Faulkener, Afzal Ahmed and Mike Brown, and to them we express our sincere appreciation.

At an early stage we were visited by Claude Janvier and had an extremely rewarding time discussing ideas and developing new ones with him. While on a visit to England, Maxim Bruckheimer read an early draft and made many valuable comments. We are very grateful to Claude and Maxim for their kind encouragement.

Our colleagues at the Open University were always at hand to discuss and argue with. We would particularly like to mention Alan Graham who listened patiently to our many tales of woe as well as of success.

PART

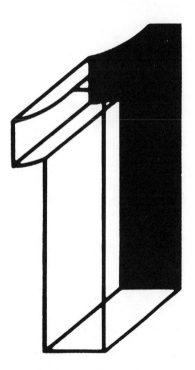

THE CLASSROOM

INTRODUCTION

— answers many of the standard questions that teachers ask before feeling ready to start on problem solving in the classroom.

At a time when there are many books available that deal with mathematical puzzles and problem solving, why produce another one? Well, we think this one is different:

• different in that it is a collection of problems varying in type, i.e. puzzles, mathematical problems, 'real' problems and investigations, all in one volume;

• different in that it confronts some of the difficulties of getting problem solving under way in schools;

• different in that its emphasis is on what students are doing, learning and feeling when they solve problems.

The book is based on our experience of working with teachers and children in a variety of schools, with children of both high and low ability, and with groups of teachers who want to add a problem solving component to their normal maths teaching.

Surprisingly, we find it makes sense to address all levels of age and attainment in the one book. We find that it doesn't matter how old or how brilliant you are, the ways in which thinking happens are common threads that reappear at all levels of problem solving. The only bias that we have taken is to set the book solidly in the context of mathematics. This is primarily because maths provides basic tools, such as calculating and graphing, that are needed in almost all problem solving activity. Also, on the other side of the coin, problem solving provides an exciting context in which mathematical activity can take place.

The book is written in two parts. This is Part 1, a

form of commentary on what we consider to be the central components of problem solving: that is, group work, emotional involvement, problem solving procedures and strategies, and classroom management. There is also a problem section, Part 2, in which we provide a number of starting points for mathematical activity. These range from puzzles to projects ... solving problems all the way.

In this introduction we describe briefly what we take problem solving to mean, why we think it important that children should work collaboratively, and what effect problem solving can have on the teacher's role in the classroom. These themes are covered in detail later in the book, but it helps initially to set the scene for what follows. We also give our reasons for being committed to problem solving in the mathematics classroom.

What is a puzzle, a project, and problem solving?

From the word go, we want to make it quite clear that 'it's not what you do, it's the way that you do it!' To say that an activity is a puzzle is more to describe the approach taken rather than the matter itself. For example, here is an introductory activity from Part 2 that has all the trappings of a puzzle.

Leap Frog

In the game of Leap Frog, the aim is to swap the positions of two sets of counters. This is the starting position

and this is the finishing position.

The counters can be moved by sliding one place into an empty position, or by jumping over another counter into the empty place.

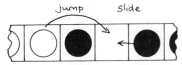

The white counters can only move to the right and the black counters can only move to the left.

If you try playing Leap Frog now, and we strongly suggest that you do, we expect you would find that:

- it is an enjoyable activity
- you will know when you have finished
- it will not take you very long to complete.

These are the main features of puzzles. Along the way, you may well have used a problem solving strategy; for example, trying a simple case is often helpful with Leap Frog, and means starting with two counters, then four and six before tackling the eight counter situation.

Leap Frog, as described above, is just the beginning of a more substantial piece of work. In Part 2 we suggest ways in which the basic game can be extended to cover more counters and different kinds of leap. The students who follow up these suggestions would be spending much more time on the Leap Frog topic and could well end up developing it into a project. Just as the English teacher is now encouraging pupils to develop, edit and present substantial pieces of writing, so the maths teacher should be developing in pupils the ability to sustain their mathematical work over longer periods and to produce accounts of their findings. This is what we mean by project work. Project work may develop from the small beginning of solving a particular puzzle, such as Leap Frog; it can also result from work that is initiated when a class realises that they share a common problem which they want to solve themselves. We call this type of work real problem solving. Examples of real problem solving are:

• organising our Sports Day;
• planning a class outing;
• what to do in wet playtimes.

Real problem solving usually extends over weeks rather than days, and involves the whole class rather than a small group of children.

Finally, whether the activity is short, like a puzzle, or extended, as in a project, or a real problem, we call it problem solving because this is our way of describing the process rather than the product of the children's work.

Why collaborative group work?

Ann considered herself to be an enlightened teacher, encouraging group work and talking, and thought she was rather good at it too, until she set about her first real problem solving project with the class of four-year-olds she had at that time. The class concerned was bored both with its classroom and with the activities offered, and wanted to improve them. She offered the children the opportunity of seeing this as a problem about which they could do something.

As they formulated this problem and later, as they split into groups to tackle aspects of it, they began to communicate with each other. They didn't just talk at each other, or pretend to listen, they actually shared ideas. They were really hearing what others had to say, expanding each other's ideas, arguing about them, defending them.

The ESL children were participating too, making contributions where they might normally have been reticent, choosing to work in an interest group rather than their ethnic group. They were being supported in their attempts in English rather than being dismissed by their peers. They were gaining confidence, and had reason and purpose in communicating. These changes in behaviour in the several years that we have been problem solving in the classroom have proved to be normal phenomena. And we have noticed it with students of all ages when they begin to work collaboratively.

5

The need to communicate and work together begins with the negotiation which the groups engage in to agree on their group goals. Having discussed what the problem is and what's involved in trying to resolve it, the pupils are then working together towards a common goal. From this stage on, the group will need to communicate, share ideas, make group decisions and keep each other informed. So, unlike much of the activity that takes place in a maths lesson, children have a real need to use the language of mathematics for communication. For example, at one report-back session, David, reporting for his group, was explaining how much polythene they would need to line the fish pond as follows:

We thought length times width would be right, but we've just read that you need to add the depth twice. That means length + depth + depth times width + depth + depth ... we think. We've done that but we're not sure we've done it right ... so we're going to use the example (holds it up) in the book to see whether we've done it right.

This sharing of ideas and information has another pay-off. Students begin naturally and spontaneously to discuss the appropriateness, efficiency and effectiveness of their methods, hypothesis testing and recommended solutions. They can see within the group how successful they are being, they know when they are satisfied with their work without constantly asking

'Is this right, Miss?'

or

'What shall I do next, Sir?'

How does this affect the teacher's role?

One thing which we found extremely difficult when we first started problem solving was taking a back seat. Even though developing the pupils' autonomy and 'let the children think' had been mottos and goals since the ivory tower days at teachers' training college, we saw in retrospect to what extent we had hindered these very processes. To a large extent we would dominate from the front, ask questions to which we already knew the answer we expected, initiate ideas and topics, and redirect pupils to take the routes that we wanted them to follow.

Imagine then how difficult we found our first few problem solving activities. For a start the problem had to belong to the students; we must not muscle in. We would see groups working well and go and interrupt with 'You look busy, what have you done so far?' Grudgingly, and very patiently, they would stop what they were doing, cease being a group and answer the question. Only five or ten minutes after we had moved away did these groups regain that degree of concentration, task directedness and group cohesion that had been disturbed.

It took us a while to learn that we were no longer essential to every move or decision that the students made. In the normal sense of 'teaching', we were not required. One felt like a fraud, anxiously looking around for someone needing help or discipline. Ann remembers well the day she decided to grit her teeth and cling to her chair resisting all temptation to disrupt the hive of industry which the class had become.

Slowly, though, came the realisation that we were not actually redundant or rendered obsolete by problem solving. Indeed, the teacher has a vital role to play. The teacher has to set up the kind of environment and atmosphere that can make this type of work possible, and be available as a resource if and when the students need help. We also found that we were free from queues of students at the desk wanting to know how or what to do, or wanting their pages of ticks or crosses. This freedom releases you and makes possible the kind of observations and diagnostic situations that mean you can really see where students' difficulties, strengths and weaknesses lie. It is then possible to plan future work for students much more realistically than in formal lessons.

Which problems will suit my class?

Part 2 of this book is a resource bank of problems that we have used in a wide range of classrooms with pupils of all ages and backgrounds. The problems themselves have not been chosen for a particular age or attainment range, the reason for this being that each individual problem can be used at a variety of levels. It is not the complexity of the problem that determines the type of solution, rather it is the approach the students take to the solution that determines its complexity.

The Bag of Sticks problem is one example of a problem able to be tackled at many levels of complexity.

Bag of Sticks

I have a bag of 12 sticks. They are all different lengths, each measuring a whole number of centimetres. I find that whenever I take three sticks out of the bag they will not make a triangle. How can this be possible?

What is the shortest possible length of the longest stick?

We presented this problem to two mixed ability classes, one of age nine, the other of age twelve. In each class, what has been described as 'the seven year gap' was evident; that is, the approaches to the problem varied from that which you might expect from a five-year-old to a sixteen-year-old student.

- For some students, the concept of triangles was limited. They explored ways of constructing triangles, discussing whether it was the space inside or the lines that made it a triangle.
- Many students began to construct triangles and thought that the solution to the problem was 12 because 'if no sticks are the same length, then 12 is the shortest you can get for the last one'. Each of the triangles they constructed was equilateral.
- One group made all their triangles isosceles, and when they drew them, the triangles all had a base that was parallel to the foot of the paper.
- Others got as far as a sequence of numbers, spotted the pattern and then could predict what length the twelfth stick would be. The problem solving skill varied enormously too, from random constructions to systematic ones starting from the first shortest possible length of stick and building upwards.
- Every group got as far as realising that if the two shorter sides were equal to the longer side, then it was not possible to make a triangle, which for some was a considerable achievement.

With such a variety of attacks on the problem being used, we began to realise that there is not something inherent in a problem that determines the kind of class for which it is suitable; rather, there is something within the problem solvers that determines the approach they will take, and that something is usually very revealing!

Why this commitment to problem solving?

Our commitment to problem solving has its roots in the classroom. Many experiences in a variety of classrooms with children aged from four to sixteen years solving various types of problems, have presented us repeatedly with surprises about what children can actually do when they are allowed to think, plan and act for themselves.

In infant classes we have seen young children reorganise their classrooms, plan assemblies and work readily with numbers 1 – 6 to solve the Magic N-grams problem. In junior classes we have seen children organising after-school clubs, planning sports days and working on spirolaterals. In secondary classes the range includes such items as Superstars Competitions, best buys and the Sticks problem.

What is not clear from these examples is the involvement that the students themselves feel when problem solving. Once the students understand that they, rather than the teacher, will be working on the problem, they display a surprising ability to think for themselves. Equally surprising is their ability to concentrate. Because having grappled with a problem to ensure that it is clear and to find the starting points, the students then become task directed. They have set goals that they want to achieve and become highly motivated to do so.

Recently a class of low attaining fourth-years

was working on a fire drill problem. One particular group contained three notoriously disruptive boys. The class teacher had felt worried about how this group would respond in this particular context, knowing that they were going to want to move around the school making drawings and taking measurements. This was a group of boys whose concentration span was short, whose motivation was usually non-existent, and with whom it was difficult to maintain discipline.

She laughed sheepishly after the lesson as she'd really underestimated those boys. They were very serious and involved with this problem. They carefully and systematically listed the routes out of school and planned how to time and measure the routes, even a method for measuring the stairs. They then not only made their measurements and timings, they also presented their findings to the rest of the class ... all without any misbehaviour.

Nor was their increased motivation and task directedness the only surprise. Only the day before this lesson the teacher had been doing a lesson on measuring. Almost every straight-edged object in the room had been measured, and not very accurately. It was of great interest to the teacher to see the ease with which the measurements were made and recorded in this real context. The greatest surprise was the level of sophistication that was brought to the problem of measuring the stairs: the discussion that led to an algorithm to use on the calculator to work out the length of 24 stairs, 27 cms wide and 19 cms deep, then the decision to divide by a hundred to convert centimetres to metres to match their measurements of the hallways, and finally the realisation that their first set of measurements might not be accurate enough, resulting in developing a double checking method.

While the students were getting ready for the final report-back session, their teacher passed us this comment from the back of the classroom.

Measurement work on "investigation" more sophisticated than in "formal" lessons → more students coping with more difficult measuring BETTER.

Sh.

This is the kind of reaction that underpins our commitment to problem solving. But what better reason could there be for wanting to share problem solving activities and experiences with other teachers than the way the students themselves feel about problem solving activities?

After we had done it I felt very pleased with myself because we had got most of the things we wanted, also because we got it all done. We all thought it was really good
Paul.

I felt very happy in what our group had done. I felt very relaxed I was glad when it was over and done with. I am satisfied with what the class has done and organised. I think our class ~~really~~ has really grown up. Helen.

— designed to help get those first two or three lessons going on problems that everyone should have success with.

Right class. Put your things down for a moment and listen to me. You've all got something to work on? (Nodded assent.) Is there anyone who's stuck? (A few hands go up.) Paul, I'll come to your group in a minute, and you Cheryl. Daniel, I'll come to your group first. The rest of you, keep going. Don't forget to make notes as you go along and be ready at the end of the lesson for someone to come and tell the rest of the class what you have found out. OK, off you go.

From that moment on, there was a gentle hum of activity. The students were working in small groups of about four or five on different problems. From time to time, one member of a group would get up to collect some paper from the cupboard, a ruler perhaps or some measuring jugs and water. The teacher moved around the classroom, sometimes answering the call of a raised hand, occasionally eavesdropping on one of the groups possibly to make notes of who was doing what, often pausing to give a friendly word of encouragement, or a suggestion as to where some item of information or resource might be found.

About ten minutes before the end of the lesson, the groups were brought together.

I hope by now that you've chosen someone to talk about what you've found out. Paul, let's start with your group.

The first group's spokesman came to the front, others soon followed. Results were drawn on the blackboard, a demonstration with jugs of water was given, diagrams handed around for everyone to see. Occasionally, a point was unclear and had to be revisited; at other times ideas for further work were suggested by the class; one of the findings was denied by the class, defended by the group and a compromise found. Then the inevitable bell went ... it felt like an unwelcome intrusion.

The lesson we have described was indeed a maths lesson. We will use it as a snapshot, something to look at while thinking about what is involved in finding a way into problem solving.

In this chapter we want to look at some of the key issues that teachers have in mind when they embark on problem solving. These issues include:

• What problems should I start the students on?
• How should I introduce the problems to the students?
• How should I handle the resources that will be needed?
• What notes should I take?

Perhaps from the outset we should make it clear that there are no recipes for instant success - are there ever in teaching? Nor does the running of a problem solving class depend on a teacher acting in any clear or hard and fast manner. But there are certain questions, such as those mentioned above, that we would like to address in order to suggest a few 'ways in'. Finally, we think it important to note that the 'way in' is to start with problem solving activities that last for no longer than a double lesson. Within that time span, there should be space for getting going, achieving results and reflecting on the outcomes.

What problems should I start the students on?

Given thirty or so students in one room, it seems unlikely that each one will want to engage with (that means get stuck into) the same problem. We have found it useful to have a selection available, and we have given below three problems, each of quite a different kind.

MacMahon's Triangles

How many different ways can you find of colouring these 3 triangles using only 2 colours?

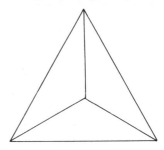

Best Magazine

If you could afford to buy only one comic or magazine a week, which would be the best value for money?

Magic N-grams

Find out how to place the numbers 1, 2, 3, 4, 5, 6, 7, 8, 9 on this triangle so that the sum of the numbers on each side is the same.

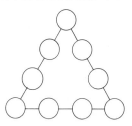

We have chosen these problems largely because each one is adaptable to a very broad age range. For example, it is not hard to imagine a group of five-year-old children working with scissors and glue on MacMahon's Triangles. Perhaps they would insist that these pictures are different.

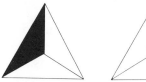

Indeed it shows quite a level of sophistication to accept that these pictures could be considered as identical. Older students' hands might shoot up quite quickly with an answer. 'What happens when you allow 3 colours?' comes the teacher's reply. For them, it would be quite a breakthrough to decide amongst themselves that it would be a good idea to find out what happens with four colours. The MacMahon's Triangle problem can also present quite a respectable challenge to even the most able of sixth-formers. Finding and proving the correctness of a formula that gives the number of distinct colourings when n colours are allowed is far from trivial.

The Best Magazine problem is again suitable for students of widely differing ages. But not as it stands. We mention it in our starter collection because of this. Young children could decide amongst themselves which was the best book in the story corner while sixth-formers might find it worthwhile to compare the facilities and programmes offered by universities and colleges of advanced education. This kind of problem obviously needs adapting to the students' interests.

Finally, we chose the Magic N-grams problem because it belongs to a fascinating group of 'Magic' problems. In its simplest form all that is needed is a smaller triangle and numbers 1 - 6.

Later, the triangle can be extended to have more spaces on each side, or the addition rule (add the numbers on each side) could be replaced by a multiplication rule. Even later, probably years later, it helps to formulate the problem algebraically as this can lead to an understanding of the properties that a given set of numbers must have before it can be used to form a magic triangle.

One of the pay-offs with problems that are so adaptable is that groups of children can each choose their own level of sophistication, the one at which they feel comfortable. This is our second reason for choosing them as starter problems. Working with a mixed-ability class, it is reassuring to know that every student should be able to achieve something by the end of a double lesson.

How should I introduce the problems to the students?

At the initial stage, it is vital to discuss with the students how problem solving might differ from their normal expectation of classroom practice. Depending on these expectations, it may be necessary to mention that:

• there is no one right answer;
• there are many different ways of approaching a problem;
• the students should decide for themselves what resources they think they will need;
• the students should discuss their ideas and findings amongst themselves;
• each group will be expected to report its results to the rest of the class at the end of the lesson, which can be very frustrating initially.

Much of this may appear to represent a change in the code of classroom behaviour. However, we like to think that there need be no change in the ground rules, or hidden curriculum; indeed working collaboratively in groups calls for substantial respect for the needs of others. Rather, the surface rules of classroom behaviour have changed in their emphasis from individual to group needs.

As you read the three starter problems, you may have reacted differently to each one. One might have been more intriguing than the rest, another more worthwhile. Students too will have these reactions. Apart from the benefits of having to negotiate a choice of problem within the group, the students may initially feel less threatened if the choice of problem is their own. Thus once the class has been divided into groups of four or five (six seems to be about the largest viable group size for this kind of work), we have found it helpful to let each group discuss and select one problem from the two or three that are offered.

With each new school and class that we worked with, we always found that pupils were initially reluctant to talk about the problem selection in their groups, didn't know what to talk about and preferred to get started independently and often half-heartedly on a problem. We think that this is partly due to the children feeling threatened by these new demands and partly to their inexperience with working collaboratively in groups.

Without some initial input from the teacher, written problem statements are seen as just another set of worksheets. Often it is necessary to arouse students' curiosity or interest in some way before introducing the problem in its written form. The following techniques for introducing problems are often useful.

1. The teacher can present the problems on an OHP, inviting students' reactions and interpretations of them, and, in some cases, rewriting and rephrasing the problems in ways that make them more appropriate to the students.

2. 'Do you know I've just spent $3.95 on a magazine and there's nothing in it but advertisements. Have you ever found that?'

3. Give the children a challenge as they read the problems. 'You think that MacMahon's Triangles looks easy, don't you. Well, I bet you can't finish it in this lesson!'

4. Encourage the children to predict or estimate how a problem will develop. For example, with Magic N-grams, you might ask the children how many different ways they think they can fit the numbers onto the diagram.

5. 'Before you are allowed to ask me anything about the problem, you have got to talk to at least two other people about it.'

After the chosen problems have been introduced in one of these ways, the children will still need some encouragement to further discuss them in their groups and to make a committed group decision as to which one to choose.

Even after introducing the problems, expect and accept initial silence; children need time and space to think. Also expect a certain amount of silliness and be patient while the pupils overcome their initial fear about getting started. Comments that it's too hard, too easy, too boring indicate that a group has not yet engaged with a problem. Here again a little teacher-pupil dialogue should soon get the group going.

If this is their first attempt at working on problem solving, you should expect the pupils to need support and direction, so be ready to get them talking. Questions such as:

'What is the problem asking you to do?'
'What might you try first?'
are helpful.

How should I handle the resources that will be needed?

Maths teaching is traditionally dominated by paper and pencil activities. Just as it is now seen as vital that students experience the learning of maths through a variety of media, from models and apparatus through to the use of calculators and microcomputers, so the students' needs in problem solving may need to be supported by access to a wide range of materials. The difficulty for the teacher is that, if the students are being asked to choose their own approach to a problem, it may prove hard to meet every need for resources. The temptation is to decide in advance on possibly appropriate resources and to impose these from the outset.

For example, how might a group of eight-year-olds decide to work on MacMahon's Triangles? We could anticipate that they might record their ideas by colouring in some prepared diagrams with red and blue crayons. This much could be provided with the problem statement. However, by making this provision, we have chosen for them the method that they will use to find a result. If this was the group's first encounter with problem solving, their real need might be to regress somewhat and spend time cutting out coloured paper triangles, getting a bit sticky with the glue pot: generally doing it their way rather than ours. Perhaps it is too easy to overlook the fact that the inhabitants of a classroom have a good notion of what resources are and are not available. They will often choose an approach that can utilise resources available from existing stock.

We have noticed another effect of giving out resources at the same time as the problem statement. Students have had years of expecting to make whatever use they can of the resources that are provided for them. If the problem involves measuring and a trundle wheel is provided, the students will use that rather than decide what is the most appropriate way of doing the measuring. As one art teacher put it, the drawback to doing 'collage' is that the medium becomes dominant over the message. First decide what you want to depict, then choose the medium that suits you best.

Of course the Best Magazine problem is different in this respect. The way in which we have stated the problem suggests that students will have to bring with them copies of any magazines that they usually read. If not carefully managed, or if the students either forget (likely) or bring undesirable magazines (even more likely), the problem solving session could be a disaster. Using this as a starter problem, therefore, probably means that the teacher will have to decide which magazines are the most appropriate for analysis. If the cost of purchase proves a barrier, it would be sensible to switch to a simpler consumer item. The only important thing is to choose something that the students are familiar with: a best buy investigation of cars in the 1100-1300 cc range would not be of any real interest to many children of school age.

In general, while it may be necessary to make available those resources that provide the starting point, we feel it important that resources that might be used on the way towards a result should not be offered explicitly. Most reasonably well stocked maths cupboards should be equipped with all the essential materials. What is important is that once a group has decided on its approach, the students should be allowed easy access to those resources that they feel will be needed.

What role should I take?

The rhythm of a problem solving class will depend very much on the role that the teacher takes.

Initially the students will need help organising themselves, even the classroom furniture, for comfortable work in groups. It is important that the groups should form themselves and not be imposed, and there are two ways in which this can happen. Initially, the students will want to work in friendship groups. Indeed, groupings of this kind are inevitable if the groups are formed before the problems are presented. However, it is our experience that subsequently students prefer to choose the problem that interests them most, without reference to their friends, and to form a group with others who are interested in the same problem area. Slowly the barriers between girls and boys, between the high and low attainers, indeed between most of the social and physical divisions that students apply to themselves, will begin to erode. But this takes time and, with the starter problems, it is best to allow such artificial barriers to remain in place.

Once the groups have been formed, it is up to the students to do the work. A distinguished teacher at the Haifa Technion, when asked what he did during his problem solving class replied, 'I read the newspaper'. Perhaps this is a bit extreme, but it is probably more enjoyable to read the newspaper than to do as one person did, namely hold onto the radiator. One way of being passively active is to work on a problem that interests you yourself. This is much the same as reading one's own book at the same time as the students are being asked to read theirs. From this, the pupils will see that you value and enjoy problem solving too, and a sense of sharing a common interest is often a valuable stimulus. The key feature is that the teacher should be approachable but not too

easily available. One needs quite a good reason for interrupting someone who is reading the newspaper.

Towards the end of the lesson, time needs to be set aside for each group to report to the rest of the class on what progress it has made with the problem. Initially, students will not feel easy about this report-back stage. They will not only find it difficult to explain their results, they will have even greater difficulty in listening to the work of others. Inaudibility and jumbled arguments are very common, and it is a great temptation for the teacher to restate loudly and clearly what a group has expressed in a mumble. To do this is to condone an unsatisfactory presentation.

During the course of a double lesson it is unlikely that each group will arrive at a neat formulation of its results exactly ten minutes before the bell rings. When a group of students announce that they have finished, it is part of the teacher's role to help them decide:

• whether they have marshalled a satisfactory argument to present their results to the rest of the class;

• whether the amount of time remaining is sufficient to pursue another aspect of the problem; or

• whether to revert to some other classwork before making their presentation.

As well as some groups finishing ahead of time, other groups may only have reached a partial conclusion by the report back time. These groups will need reminding to break off and prepare their report even though it may be incomplete.

After the lesson

When the lesson is over, it can be quite fascinating to look back over what has taken place. This need not take long, but, as memory is such a fragile faculty, it is worth recording some immediate impressions on which to build next time. Questions that can be asked include:

- How well were the problems presented?
- Did the groups work collaboratively?
- Were the resources adequate?
- What did I learn about my role?
- Were there any surprises or disappointments?
- What would I do differently next time?

However, it would be premature to start coming to any hard and fast conclusions at this stage. The students are beginners just as much as the teacher, and their confidence and ability will be at a very early stage of development.

WORKING IN A GROUP 2

— explains the early frustrations and later bonuses that come with small group work

There are lots of things that we'd like to tell you about group work, but that doesn't feel like the right approach somehow. Instead we're going to talk about the changes and reactions that one particular class of ten-year-old children experienced as a result of collaboratively solving problems. From this account of observations made as part of our research, you can draw your own conclusions.

When we first met this particular class of students, they had no experience of problem solving or of working collaboratively in groups. The first task was to select the problem to work on. This was chosen by the class and was to be 'to organise a class Christmas party'. After an initial brainstorming session, the class divided into five groups to cover catering, costing, entertainment, timetabling and decorations. The groups took responsibility for their allotted area and the final solution that was put into action was truly a group effort.

The early stages

Our observations in the early stages highlighted areas of confusion which were causing major difficulty to the children. The first of these was that they were not convinced that they were going to choose the problem and that they would be allowed to put their chosen solution into action. They found it difficult to believe that they would be making the decisions and not the teacher, and particularly that they were responsible for what would happen and must think for themselves.

Evidence of teacher dependence was frequent and manifest. This took the form of questions to the teacher such as 'Can we have a ...?' or 'Are we allowed to ..?'. It was also demonstrated by individuals making repeated eye contact with the teacher, to ensure that their ideas and comments were accepted and approved by the teacher, rather than by the rest of the class who, in this instance, were the important audience and judge.

An important part of group problem solving work is the ability and willingness of students to generate ideas about what is involved in the problem. Their inexperience at generating ideas in a non-judgemental way resulted in hesitancy, reluctance by some children to generate ideas at all, and also in the generation of silly or impractical ideas.

When the people from the Open University came they asked Mr Adams to set a problem for the class to do for Christmas so we told them our suggestions. Some of them were impossible to do and some were good. We crossed off the ones that were impossible and then we crossed off some more and finally we ended up with four good suggestions.
Helena

As confidence began to develop, however, the ease with which the relevant ideas were generated was greatly improved.

In the time that we were given we all made suggestions, some of the suggestions that were sensible were kept and thought about, but most of the ideas were rejected as they were too ambitious. The class agreed that our aim was "To make almost everybody satisfied". We split up into groups, the groups were called, Party, Christmas Tree, Decorations and Christmas Cards.

Alexandra Pryor.

The child's role in the class

This being a truly mixed-ability class, it had two or three bright sparks who tended to dominate discussions and produce 'right' answers quickly in traditional lessons. One would tend to describe them as over-confident, even precocious. At the other end of the spectrum were the low attainers and a very withdrawn child, each of whom either tried to be totally inconspicuous, never contributing to a class discussion, or else was disruptive when bored. In the middle, of course, were those few who worked laboriously, contributing occasionally, but often unnoticeably. Each had a view of his role in the class.

During the first few problem solving sessions these roles were largely maintained within the small groups. As the children began to 'engage' with the problem, they began to have things to say, things that the rest of the group needed to hear and attend to. One example of this was when Claire, a normally reticent child, didn't like the plan that her group (the party catering group) was making for food and drinks. She was quite cross when she said, almost in tears,

> That's not fair. I don't like strawberry squash and I don't like salt and vinegar crisps and by the time you've got all that chocolate and stuff we'll all be sick. I think it's babyish and we should ask everyone in the class what they like.

She didn't add 'so there ugh!', but it wasn't far away.

This had set the cat amongst the pigeons. The rest of the group could see her point but didn't want to. They discussed it and argued about it and finally concluded that it was everybody's party so it had to be made fair. Claire had won in two senses. She'd not only won her point, she'd won a certain prestige she'd never had before. The group began to look to her for ideas and approval. This wasn't the only occasion of this nature, and as the year progressed, group dynamics changed frequently as each child was discovered to have some special quality or propensity that had never had a chance to come to the fore in class work before. Interestingly too, those who in the formal class work had looked like natural leaders were not necessarily the group's chosen leaders. Nor did those who seemed bright in normal lessons dominate the groups; they had things to learn about problem solving too. With each problem the group dynamics vary ... most children get to drive at some time and most get to sit in the back seat occasionally, but they all have a vital part to play within the group and in the overall solution to a problem.

Listening to others

Another major difficulty observed was in the area of communication, that is in listening, speaking objectively, putting forward a case, sharing ideas, accepting another point of view, etc. Great frustration was experienced, therefore, in group and class work where it was necessary to sort out areas of disagreement, to put forward reasons supporting statements or suggestions or retreating from an earlier point of view without apparent loss of face.

Actually working together in these groups and collaborating on a common task also produced difficulties because most children were only accustomed to working individually. Similarly, at report-back sessions it was difficult for the working groups to listen to each other's ideas. This aspect was vital if the groups were to get an overview of the problem and how each group's facts fitted together to form a solution to the overall challenge.

A context for language development

An obvious advantage of group work is the scope it provides for sharing ideas and hence for language work. At first, students put into groups and expected to talk find it difficult, and especially so in mathematics classes. Much of mathematics work is done silently, in isolation. Pupils are told what to do and expected to get on with it. They have little opportunity for clarifying ideas or using the language of mathematics.

Collaborative group work is an active process. If the group is to proceed at all, it has got to talk. It must talk about the problem, the strategies that might be useful, the way to get started or what a solution might look like; and each person's ideas must be attended to. There are many hurdles along this road to collaboration. One such hurdle arises when students have an idea or think they've just had an insight which they wish to share with the group. They begin tentatively, 'No ... I don't think ... um ... They don't want to all be the same length ... One strip of crepe gets folded round ... right ... it ... um ... needs to be longer ... umm ... twice as long ... it goes round twice ... see'.

Then, after some groping and grappling, the words are found, thinking is clarified, not just for the benefit of others but also for oneself. It's quite a common experience to think, 'Good, I've got it', and then when trying to explain, to realise that you haven't quite got it after all. That kind of realisation

might never happen; the idea could be lost or stored incomplete in memory without an attempt to verbalise it.

Frequently a group member will have an idea that conflicts with the rest of the group. This might cause frustrations and tensions. Early on in group work the students may not have the required emotional maturity or linguistic repertoire to cope with these minor crises. The art of persuasion, presenting a case and making a point, has not been given scope to develop. This was a noticeable change with this class. There was no such thing as objective discussion when such a crisis occurred, rather there was heated unstructured argument. Biased, unsupported statements met inflexible listeners, and neither side would move. Any attempts at persuasion were based on limited data and lack of relationships within the argument.

Having reached just such an impasse, one group saying that they wanted party games and the others arguing for a disco at the Christmas party, no headway could be made. Eventually, one group member suggested that if each group presented some facts and data, their cases could then be presented to the class for a vote. This was the first instance of logical debate. Within a very short space of time both cases were presented, both seen as essential ingredients of a party, and the timetabling group got the job of ensuring that there was time/space at the party for both. Both sides had learnt a lot. Reflecting on this problem later, the groups concerned reported that they had learned that 'arguing gets you nowhere except cross'. They thought they'd been babyish and that in future they'd try to get all their facts straight first and then convince others in their group without fighting. The beginnings of negotiation and seeing each other's points of view were underway.

That is not to say that, as the problem unfolded, there were no instances of students being unwilling or unable to see somebody else's point of view. Often personal experience, expectation, bias or fantasy would act as a block. The student would become rigid, inflexible, refusing to give way or try to fit in with the group. At this stage, negotiation skills and objectivity were completely lacking.

The project outcome

Having put their solution into action and experienced tremendous success in the form of the best Christmas party ever, the children were ready to reflect on what they had done in their groups, as is demonstrated by the extracts shown below.

My Contribution was cheese and I think we got to the target To make almost everybody satisfied"
Samantha. S

When we were making them I felt very proud to be helping our class in an achievment and I was very pleased to be in that group with all my best friends.
Susan.

When the party was over I felt pleased that it had been such a success. I liked our own party more than the 4th year's party because in our own party we all contributed to it and we all made some decisions.
Jayne.

Making progress

Fresh from this success the children were keen to try some other problems. Their next experiences were with Magic N-grams (see Chapter 1) and Paper Folding.

Paper Folding

Fold a piece of paper in half. Then make one more fold through the crease. Now cut in a straight line.

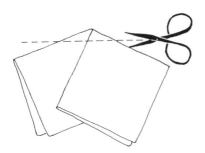

What shapes can you make in this way?

Their first experience of problem solving in groups had evidently brought about changes in the pupils' expectations. They didn't look worried faced with these problem statements, nor did they wait for teacher guidance.

'Right, let's discuss what this problem's about!'

was the immediate reaction of one group, without the teacher having to say anything. They did discuss the problems too, much less self-consciously than they had the time before. They made sure that they understood what the problems meant, rephrasing them in terms that they could associate with, and then repeating the new statements as if sticking them in memory. By this time each group had decided which problem it was going to work on and had set a group goal or challenge. No one looked to the teacher for approval or asked 'Is this what we were meant to do?'.

In one group working on the Magic N-grams it was agreed that members would try different ways and then compare their ideas with those of the rest of the group. Comments such as 'Well, if you use all the big numbers in one row, it won't work will it? You've got to sort of share them out a bit, big, medium, little, get it?' were offered, sometimes extended, and accepted. Occasionally, an attempt to explain to a group would result in a student realising why something didn't work or how it could be improved upon. These minor setbacks didn't seem too daunting for these children when shared in the group.

For the groups working on paper folding the pattern was different. At first there was no talk of strategy or working together. Scissors and paper in hand, the cutting and folding began individually amid occasional comments of 'I've made a sort of arrowhead', responded to in the 'So have I, that's easy' fashion. Many arrowheads and a few quadrilaterals were aimlessly cut before Tania announced,

'You can only make four-sided shapes.'

and wrote down

'Two folds + one cut = four sides'.

The group members were in agreement and were about to consider the problem finished when Jason said

'Hang about, I've just cut a triangle.'

Stunned silence, and disappointment, but not for long:

'What other shapes are there?'
'Let's try and cut a square.'

Only now was the work load shared as they talked about places to fold and places to cut and each agreed to try for different shapes. Now they folded, but opened up, displayed and discussed the method and outcome. Collaboration was underway, they were now task-directed. At last they had a challenge, to try to fold a square, kite and parallelogram and, if possible, to try to predict which folds and cuts would produce what shape. It wasn't long either before this initial success led them to reformulate their goal and go for three folds and one cut. They were trying now to predict the number of sides and types of shapes their efforts would produce. They weren't, however, being systematic in their search, nor were they sorting out their examples as they went along. Their efforts were all in a heap, along with the off-cuts.

At the end of this session each group was to present its solution and reasoning for it to the rest of the class. This was rather poorly done, the groups were still not very good at listening to each other, or were smug about their own ideas and methods. The explanations themselves were rather weak: mainly descriptive rather than explanatory, and often shyly mumbled. Other groups hadn't really listened so they didn't have any comments or questions to raise. Since this is not something that

was a normal part of their school work, it was hardly surprising that the children were poor at it at this early stage.

Developing responsibility

One of the things that is particularly striking about collaborative group work is its natural rhythm. There are times when concentration is intense, often for quite long periods (more than the 10 minute span that students are frequently credited with). These periods of intensity, however, are frequently followed by some frivolity and light relief. In the early problem solving days we used to feel tempted to intervene, to check this light-heartedness, but realise now that's not the thing to do. If the pupils have really taken the problem on board, engaged with it, and negotiated their goals, there will be long periods of task-directedness. These will be followed by brief spells of disengaging from the problem. But the commitment earlier established will not be lost. After a few minutes' distraction, someone within the group usually says

'Come on, let's get this finished.'

or makes a comment to draw attention back to the task in hand, and that is enough; the group get themselves back to work without teacher interference.

Already then there were signs of the children in our research class taking responsibility, thinking for themselves, talking to each other, sharing ideas and making mistakes in the support of their own group. It is strange really how very supportive and protective of each other the children are once the group becomes cohesive. There were some signs too of objectivity beginning to develop, rather than arguments stubbornly or noisily given for a particular point of view; techniques to convince or persuade were being developed.

With each new group problem solving experience these children 'grew', began to take on new roles, revised their expectations about what learning was and their role in the process. They began to apply these changes in other areas of the curriculum and with other teachers. One teacher trying to get the children working on a 'canal' project had his lesson taken over. The children told him that they should brainstorm the project, see what was involved in it and that it would then be better if they worked in groups on each aspect to share the workload. They also had big ideas for doing something with their work ... they wanted the whole of the corridor for displays. Thinking and taking responsibility had become an expectation for these pupils. Other teachers who came into contact with this class began to comment about their level of maturity and ability to get on.

What more can be said about this class except that their motivation and autonomy changed enormously as a result of their group work. This displayed itself in the way they settled down to work without constant attention from the teacher, in the way they took initiatives and made decisions with

confidence, and in the way they disciplined themselves. They wanted to accomplish their tasks, so they dealt with any disruptions to their flow due to any lack of discipline within the group.

We said at the beginning of this chapter that we would leave you to draw your own conclusions, but all that we seem to have done is present our own. In a sense that's deliberate; we're not asking you to just believe all we've said with no evidence of your own. If you've tried it, you'll have supporting evidence for these conclusions. If you haven't tried it, you'll have the evidence for your own conclusions when you do.

Other benefits of collaborative group work

In addition to mathematical puzzles and investigations, Part 2 of this book also contains examples of mini-problems and 'real' problems. A special feature of these is the role that they can play in multi-cultural classrooms. Much of what is presented in the mathematics curriculum is based on a Western top down approach, in which the curriculum demands of the following year shape the current year's syllabus. The result is that the curriculum bears little relationship to the lives of many white English-speaking children, let alone to the multi-cultural classes that most schools have.

In real problem solving it is the class that generates a real problem so the interests, experiences and preferences of the whole class are represented in the choosing of a problem. In this way these problems are not non-racist, trying not to represent any cultural bias (as much that goes on in school tries to be). Rather, it is multi-racist in a way that allows the background and culture of each member of the class to be utilized and valued.

Mini-problems and real problems both draw on the students' background when the problem factors are discussed. An example of this is the Best Magazine problem.

Best Magazine

If you could afford to buy only one comic or magazine a week, which would be the best value for money?

Multi-cultural classes working on this problem generated ideas about what they liked and disliked in magazines. Not only did these ideas differ between boys and girls but also between cultural backgrounds. Statements arose about what was omitted that made magazines of less interest to some. Similarly, issues about the type of people represented were highlighted when the problem statement was changed to

'What kind of magazine would have something for all our class?'

What we have found most exciting, then, is the way in which cultural interests and backgrounds are brought into problem solving work. These are not imposed, but brought forward naturally by the children themselves. Just as listening to others' ideas can develop in collaborative group work, so can a much greater understanding of another's cultural background.

The question of equal opportunities, girls and maths, has not been addressed specifically, but before concluding this chapter, it's worth mentioning that problem solving does have a role to play in breaking through the barriers that girls all too frequently feel concerning mathematics. The least it can offer is a fresh start: opportunities for girls to use the maths that they feel comfortable with. From this comes an element of success which will demonstrate to the girls that they can do maths and from which they can then build. Just as the problem solving approach can offer opportunities for multi-cultural children to participate and use their experiences, so can it for girls too.

3 FEELINGS WILL BE AROUSED

— almost unheard of, but true, real emotions will be aroused in the maths classroom when problem solving gets under way.

The initiator of so much recent activity in the field of problem solving, George Polya, wrote:

> The essential ingredient of a problem is the desire, the will and the resolution to solve it.

In the previous chapter there is the suggestion that the power of the group dynamic itself generates many positive feelings and attitudes towards problem solving. In this chapter we will focus more on the individual and consider the way in which problem solving induces feelings in each participant. First we will look at feelings of frustration, seeing how these might arise. For example, this is how one ten-year-old talked about

her work on the Christmas party problem that we introduced in the previous chapter.

Decorations

First we decided what group we were going to be in. I decided to be in the decorations group. Then we thought of crepe paper (twisted), disco paper cut into thin strips and folded into zig zag. we thought of a hoop in the middle of the room to fix all the decorations to the hoop. Then we did a survey to see how many people agreed but not everyone did so Claire helped me to change it abit ~~change it abit~~. But we didn't agree. By this time I was getting quite mad so I ripped it up and Justine went into another group and we forgot about it.

by Tracy

Next we want to consider the kinds of anxiety that students may feel. At times problem solving can be a threatening activity and this needs to be balanced by allowing students to find their own level within the problem, to feel at ease or comfortable.

What we hope to show is that after repeated exposure to problem solving work, the negative emotions of frustration and anxiety, which are all too frequently felt in maths lessons, can be balanced or cancelled out by the more positive emotions of satisfaction and feeling comfortable. This shift in emotions leads, we have found, to a considerable improvement in students' self-concept. The feelings seem to change from a sense of 'I don't, therefore I can't' to the more positive feeling of 'I do, therefore I can'. Alongside this growth of self-concept we have also noticed an increase in the students' sense of autonomy. Far greater willingness is shown by them to plan their own actions and to shoulder responsibility for their own decisions. After only two terms of problem solving work, Paul, aged nine, wrote:

> After we had done it
> I felt very pleased with myself because we had got most of the things we wanted, also because we got it all done. We all thought it was really good
> Paul.

What happens when pupils don't engage with the problem?

A group of twelve-year-olds had chosen to work on the following problem.

Paper Folding

Fold a piece of paper in half. Then make one more fold through the crease. Now cut in a straight line.

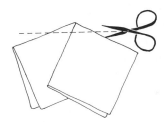

What shapes can you make in this way?

After about ten minutes of fairly noisy activity, the first paper dart came heading across the classroom. Clearly something was wrong. The teacher decided to let them have their heads for a few minutes longer, hoping that either they would pull themselves out of their obvious sense of frustration or that she would get there before the situation got too fraught with emotions. It was soon clear that an intervention was needed. As she was talking to the group, calming them down, two remarks were made which seemed to epitomise their feelings:

> Please Miss, Ajay says you have to fold it like this. But his doesn't look like it says on the paper.

and

> Look it doesn't seem to make any difference, you always get an arrow, so what's the point anyway.

The first of these remarks is typical of the frustration that can arise when a problem has not been taken on board. There are references to external authorities, often of the kind, 'What do they want us to do?' or 'That's not how they want us to do it'. It seems that the problem is still outside the problem solver. The feeling that the problem is imposed or still belongs to an outside authority often leads to a sense of frustration which, in turn, shows up in lack of involvement. What is needed is to help the students to really understand what is problematic, to feel that they know or at least recognise the obstacles that the problem poses. They need to make the problem their own, to have it inside them.

The second remark highlights another source of anxiety that can arise as students begin to engage with a problem. If the activity is seen as having no point or if the students get the feeling that they have been asked to do the impossible, it will be unlikely that they will get going. Thus a vital early stage in problem solving is to find a purpose. Each individual needs to share the purpose, to feel that the activity has a goal and that there is something that needs to be discovered or resolved. To reach this common understanding takes time.

Initially, it comes as something of a shock to students to find that the work they have been asked to do is not clearly defined. In almost every subject area, the students expect to face well-defined tasks, both in terms of the outcome and in the method to be used. It is an anxious time for them when they are unable to find the activity's purpose, made all the more difficult by their not being accustomed to this stage of problem solving. However, once this stage has been accomplished, we have repeatedly seen how each person within a group begins to settle down and feel at ease with the prospect ahead. Because the decision to pursue a particular line of investigation has been accepted by each member, the task becomes possible. Also, subsequent activity makes sense to the students as they can see the purpose in what they are doing.

The excitement of insight

Our six-year-old daughter asked Johnny, 'Daddy, have your eyes ever been checked?' Well, he wears glasses so he wondered why she should ask him a question like that — maybe the school had just had a visit from an optician. •

'Yes, of course they have', he replied.
'No they haven't. They've always been blue.'

was her comeback. And she laughed at how easy it had been to catch him out. She laughed and was happy, even a bit excited. What is it about a joke that gets us? It must have something to do with that flipover from 'Now I don't get it' to 'Now I do'. And isn't this what we mean by insight?

Insight is what happens to us when a foggy state of not knowing suddenly changes to a clear sense of being sure. Interestingly enough, this change of state is called insight and not outsight. Insight is definitely something that happens within; both the confusion and the clarity are within as well!

But what have jokes got to do with mathematics? Well, first of all, children's fascination with jokes, even in their first days at school, shows that they are ready for insight. They love telling jokes and repeating them endlessly. That is, they bring with them to school the experience of insight. Secondly, the pleasure of having insight is one that stays with us all our lives. And lastly, almost all mathematical activity has at its core the need for insight, which Martin Gardner made the subject of his book *The AHA Experience*.

In England, the Open University Maths Summer Schools hold mathematical nightclubs, largely as a way of helping the students to share the insight experience. Actually highlighting it in this way makes insight an experience that students can learn to recognise in themselves, which is important because so few students, whether adults or children, are aware of insight when it happens to them.

We also remember once watching a fifteen-year-old in a low-ability class struggling with this problem.

Eureka!

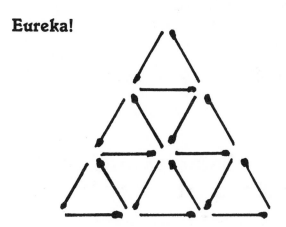

Take away 6 matches to leave only 3 triangles.

For about 20 minutes she worked on seemingly endless combinations of 6 matches to take away. Then all of a sudden the answer was there. She had got it. But it was what happened next that we found more exciting than watching the breakthrough. For the next 15 minutes or so, Francine repeated the solution of the problem. First she did it alone for herself. Then she showed it to other pupils in the class. Each time you could see the excitement with which she relived that moment of insight.

In Part 2 of this book you will find two topics that look a bit different to the rest. These are 'Eureka' and 'I've Got a Rule'. Neither are intended to lead to any serious mathematical investigation. They are included merely as very short activities that foster the experience of insight. If you decide to use them, do it sparingly, but each time give the children a chance to reflect on their own personal moment of insight. We have seen lots of children do this and then gradually carry their understanding through to problem solving in a more mathematical context.

What obstacles am I likely to meet on the way?

As work on the problem progresses, it is also possible for frustration to enter in. In the previous chapter we mentioned the difficulty that individuals can experience when they feel that the group's efforts are not going in their preferred direction, or that the results do not look like coming out in the way that they want. This was highlighted by Tracy's remarks at the beginning of this chapter. It is equally frustrating for the individuals to find that they are unable to express their ideas in a way that makes sense to other people. This is an extremely common source of anxiety in problem solving. Often students have a feeling that they can see what is wanted, but are unable to talk about

their ideas in a convincing manner. As a result, they may well appear to withdraw from the group until their ideas have become sufficiently well formulated to allow them to be expressed clearly.

To illustrate these two sources of anxiety, let's pick up the example mentioned earlier — the Paper Folding problem. The group had eventually established that they were going to look at what happened when the second fold was made at different angles. Ajay felt that they ought to make a chart of what they found out and was working on producing a table on which to record results.

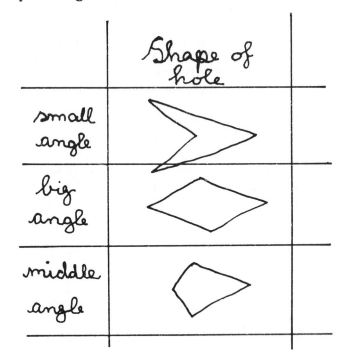

His problem was that the rest of the group were folding and cutting at such a rate that he was unable to keep track of the shapes that were being collected. He had a clear direction in which he wanted to go but was unable to convince the group that he was on to something. They seemed content to go on cutting, comparing and collecting more and more shapes ... which left Ajay out in the cold. He soon lost interest in the work and began to fool about.

Tina, meanwhile, had spotted that at a certain stage, the figures stopped looking like squares and began to look like arrowheads. Somewhere in between she could see that two sides of four-sided figures would make a straight line. This would make a ... she probably couldn't remember the right word. Excitedly she tried to explain her insight to the group.

'Look, when you go down and don't go too far it goes different.'

Her excitement was met by blank faces, and you could see her enthusiasm waning rapidly.

Having mentioned these two emotional obstacles that students are likely to meet, we have to say that these pale into insignificance before the most common cause of frustration in problem solving — teacher interference.

The problem with teacher interference is that it is so seldom intentional. The last time it happened to Johnny was with a group of trainee-teachers who were working on the following problem.

Stamps (from Weighing it Up)

Using only 5 cent and 7 cent stamps, what postage amounts can you stick on a letter?

One group had amassed a great quantity of background results but was finding that the information 'wouldn't speak to them'. All he said was,

'What happens if you multiply those two numbers?'

You could almost hear the penny drop, and it wasn't a particularly nice sound. After all their work on producing the information, he had snatched the moment of glory from them. In Chapter 6 we will be looking at the teacher's role in problem solving in detail; at this stage we would only want to alert you to the fact that the teacher can so easily, even with the best intentions, become a source of frustration to students.

A sense of satisfaction

To counteract the frustrations and anxieties that will arise during the course of problem solving activity, there is a great sense of satisfaction that it can generate. In particular, students often feel very pleased with their efforts when they find that their solutions are accepted and confirmed by others, both within their group and by the rest of the class.

Also notable is their pleasure in using mathematics effectively to achieve their goals. Frequently, the level of mathematics may not be as sophisticated as it might be. That is, students often seem to regress in the mathematical ideas that they choose to use. What happens is that, rather than use a technique that is newly learned and with which they do not feel thoroughly at home, students will frequently fall back on a method that is comfortable to them. As an example, here is an account of a piece of work produced by an eleven-year-old.

Working in the Food group for the year group disco, Brian had been given a rather responsible job — costing and buying the bread. After discussing the problem with his Mum in the evening he came back to school with this clear statement of the relevant information:

Number of children   84
Cost of loaf   97 cents
Each child eats   4 slices
Number of slices
   in a loaf   22

At this point Brian regressed – he was afraid to do the calculations such as 84×4 by long multiplication for fear of getting the wrong answer. But he found a way through:

$$\begin{array}{r} 84 \\ +\ 84 \\ \hline 168 \end{array} \qquad \begin{array}{r} 168 \\ +\ 84 \\ \hline 252 \end{array} \qquad \begin{array}{r} 252 \\ +\ 84 \\ \hline 336 \end{array}$$

To divide by 22, he again dropped back to earlier methods:

$$10 \times 22 = 220$$

$$\begin{array}{r} 220 \\ +\ 22 \\ \hline 242 \end{array} \qquad \begin{array}{r} \overset{4}{2}22 \\ +\ 22 \\ \hline 204 \end{array} \qquad \begin{array}{r} 264 \\ 22 \\ \hline 286 \end{array}$$

$$\qquad 11 \qquad\qquad 12 \qquad\qquad 13$$

$$\begin{array}{r} 286 \\ +\ 22 \\ \hline 308 \end{array} \qquad \begin{array}{r} 308 \\ +\ 22 \\ \hline 330 \end{array} \qquad \text{Next one will do}$$

$$\qquad 14 \qquad\qquad 15$$

Later, one member of the Food group said he could have used a calculator, but Brian was happy that he had found the right answer in his own way.

What happens if they get stuck?

Inevitably there will be times when, despite carefully laid plans, the students get stuck, involved in a line of investigation that is leading nowhere, or meet unforeseen obstacles in work outside the classroom. Initially this feeling of being stuck can lead to frustration or a sense of disaffection with the problem. This was particularly evident in Geoffrey's group (it was called Geoffrey's group because he was by far the tallest). They were trying to prove that a particular stretch of road was a dangerous place for a school pedestrian crossing. Their first notion was that more likely than not the local drivers would be breaking the speed limit. The group was able to take a survey, thanks to the presence of an auxiliary teacher who was available to supervise. They worked accurately with tape measures and stop watches and produced the following bar chart.

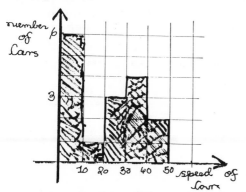

After such painstaking work they were very disappointed to find that not only were there no examples of speeding but that the vast majority of drivers were driving very safely, at less than 40 km/h. The group felt really stuck; they had wanted to show one thing and seemed to have proved the opposite. Their frustration showed itself in surly, disruptive behaviour, and it wasn't until another student in the class pointed out a way past the difficulty that they resumed normality. It was the cars in the 0-10 km/h range that were causing the problem. They were not moving at all but were dangerously parked thus causing a hazard to any children trying to see if cars were approaching. What was interesting was that, having experienced the frustration of being stuck, Geoffrey's group worked all the harder when they found the way through.

Coming face to face with the outside world can also cause difficulties. A frequent problem is that students fail to think ahead and things don't go quite as planned.

Who Can Tell?

Can't people tell one brand of crisps from another? Devise an experiment to find out.

One group that tackled this problem set it up as a competition between two classes. The experiment was to be held over break and a parallel class was challenged to see which was the more discerning. In the rush of trying to manage sixty people to undergo a fairly rigorous tasting exercise, things started to go wrong. By the time break was over, only half the data had been collected and two bags of crisps had gone missing. Perhaps the most important lesson this group learned was that they had no-one to blame but themselves, but this didn't stop them from experiencing a period of anger and disappointment before they were able to plan the exercise successfully.

When a student gets stuck, there is very likely to be an accompanying sense of failure, disappointment or frustration. But should these feelings be avoided? Can the experience not be put to good use? We believe it can and have seen many examples where the breakthrough leads to a much greater sense of responsibility and ultimate achievement. One of the hardest lessons to be learned in problem solving is that mistakes are going to be made.

What happens if there is no conclusion?

Let us begin by saying that lack of a conclusion or even partial resolution appears to be the least cause of anxiety amongst students. First of all, it is not a particularly common occurrence, especially as work started in one lesson can often be carried over to the next. Secondly, once a start has been

made the greatest barrier has been crossed, and the work that follows is likely to be carried out at the level at which individuals feel comfortable.

We have, however, noticed that, if two groups are working on the same problem, there is what appears to be a sense of competition between the groups. On the other hand, it is not our experience that this leads to a demoralisation of the group that fails to 'get so far', probably because each member of each group has been able to become involved; the sense of achievement seems to override any disappointment that one might expect them to feel.

To conclude this chapter, we would like to return to the notion that the most important feature of problem solving is the resolve and will to find a solution. Inevitably, once a sense of commitment has been made, any stumbling blocks along the way are likely to lead to anxiety or frustration. These negative emotions can initially deter students from keeping going. But the stronger the emotions are, the more pleasing and satisfying are the emotions felt at the end. Both aspects, we believe, have a vital role to play, not only during the activity of problem solving but also subsequently as the students' self-concept grows and their sense of autonomy develops.

WHAT WILL HAPPEN

— the major stages of problem solving are outlined, from initial problem identification through to reviewing what has been achieved.

When children are working on a project or a real problem, their activity often follows a pattern. The first stage involves defining the areas that they will investigate. This is followed by small group work on various aspects of the problem; and finally ideas and findings are put together either to form a report or to lead on to some kind of action. In the literature about problem solving, many different models or 'heuristics' of the process are given, but on close examination these heuristics have a lot in common. Our preferred way of describing what happens in problem solving is the PROBLEMS acronym. This acronym is shorthand for the following list of steps:

Pose the problem

Refine into areas for investigation

Outline the questions to ask

Bring the right data home

Look for solutions

Establish recommendations

Make it happen

So what next?

In this chapter we want to flesh out what the PROBLEMS model means, show how it relates to different levels of problem solving activity, and finally suggest ways in which it can be used to guide the approach that you take to problem solving with your class.

An example of the PROBLEMS heuristic

First, then, we include an account of real problem solving that Ann carried out with her class of nine-year-old children.

PLAYTIME

Pose the Problem

For some time, my class had been reluctant to go out to play, and tried to find excuses not to go out at playtimes. I had also noticed that there had been many instances of children from other classes coming into school for petty reasons during breaks. As the situation seemed to get no better, I asked my class what they thought the reasons were. A long list of ideas about what was wrong with playtimes was soon generated and recorded on the board.

Things we don't like about playtime
- It's boring
- Nothing to play with - no amusements
- You can only run around
- Other schools have things to play on
- Bikes not allowed in the playground
- Waiting in line is boring
- Want more things to do
- Lose things at playtime — vandalism
- Bushes get damaged
- Not allowed on the grass
- Footballs are dangerous
- Playground too crowded
- Use more of the school's entrances and exits
- Bullying
- Coats — cloakroom's too small

As these ideas were recorded, my class got very involved and decided that, if I would let them, they really could do something to improve playtime.

Refine into areas for investigation

The next step was to try to sort out the ideas and refine them into areas to investigate. The topic web on the next page was the result of a fairly lengthy class discussion, which concluded with the children deciding that their challenge was 'to make the playground less boring'.

Outline the questions to ask

The children soon knew which groups they wanted to work in and went off in these groups to discuss exactly what their area for investigation involved. At first, they did not find it easy to decide what questions they needed to ask. The 'It's boring' group knew that they wanted things to play with, but did not know what to suggest to overcome this difficulty. I asked what they thought the

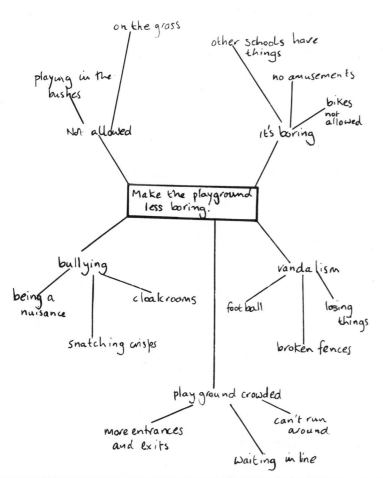

on the grass

other schools have things

no amusements

playing in the bushes

bikes not allowed

Not allowed

it's boring

Make the playground less boring.

bullying

vandalism

being a nuisance

cloakrooms

football

losing things

snatching crisps

broken fences

playground crowded

can't run around

more entrances and exits

waiting in line

most popular playtime activities would be, and what other children might like to do at playtimes. They said they did not know, so I asked how they might find out.

'Oh,' said Edward, 'I know. We could do a survey and when we've found out we could take some action and write a letter to the council to ask if we could change our playground.'

The penny had dropped and they explained to the rest of the class what they had thought of. I wrote their idea on the board as an 'if...then' statement. This helped the other groups and resulted in the following table.

Group	If we knew ...	... then we could
It's boring	what people liked	take some action and write a letter to the local council to ask if we could change our playground.
	what was the most popular	see how much it costs, and begin to make plans.
Vandalism (also tidying up the fence)	who vandalised the fence	try to stop them.
Bullying	who bullies most	report the bullies to the Head.

39

Group	If we knew ...	... then we could
	where bullying happens	have teachers watch the spots where bullying happens most.
Playground	that the playground was too crowded that people wanted a quiet area	write to the council for planning permission. try to split the playground up.
Not allowed	if people want to play on the grass and sand	ask permission and try and get some support.

4. Barrels and things

5. A quiet area

6. A place for playing marbles or cars

7. A place to ride bikes

8. A place for rough games

Look for solutions ('It's boring' group only)

When this group had collected and analysed their data, they announced to the class that climbing frames and a place for marbles or cars were the two most popular. This news was greeted with groans and protests from most of the girls and some of the boys in the class. When asked what they were complaining about, it became apparent that everybody had filled in the questionnaire even though they did not like the choices on it. A wide range of popular activities was then suggested by the rest of the class. The five boys in the 'It's boring' group had listed on the questionnaire only those things that interested them. They were forced to realise their error, and rewrote their questionnaire to ask what all pupils would most like to have in the playground.

Look for solutions (the whole class)

When each of the groups had collected, analysed and interpreted their data, I asked each group to report their solutions to the rest of the class. These are listed on the page opposite.

Bring the right data home ('It's boring' group only)

The 'It's boring' group wanted to know what activities people would like, and thought a questionnaire would be the best way of collecting the data that they needed. The questionnaire that they designed is shown below.

Which of these would you like in our playground? You can choose three.

1. Climbing frames

2. Swings

3. Roundabouts

Vandalism group
We need more litter bins at specific points.

We should stop people going over the fence to fetch footballs.

We should have a stronger fence.

We should inform the school (in assembly and using posters) that keeping the school and playground tidy is important.

We should tell teachers who goes over the fence.

Not allowed group
We should ask the Head if people can play on the grass in fine weather.

Football should be banned because the playground is too small.

We should display posters of the school rules.

Football could be played on the field.

Bullying group
We should tell teachers who the bullies are.

We should tell teachers where bullying happens most.

We should write a report about bullying and read it at assembly.

We should ask the teachers to watch the bullying blackspots at playtimes.

We should have two teachers on duty if all the corners and things are to be watched.

The playground should be split into two so that football (footballers are the worst bullies) can be played in only one part of it.

Playground is crowded group

We should split the playground into two parts, one for rough games and one for quiet games.

We should ask the local council if we can make the playground bigger by using some of the field.

It's boring group

We should have an adventure playground.

We should try to get permission from the council for an adventure playground.

We should set up an area for quiet games at playtime.

I was pleased with their progress to this point, but there was still a long way to go before they could make anything happen.

Establish recommendations

From the lists of recommendations the class realised that there were conflicts (football should be banned versus playground split into two) and overlaps (one part for rough games and one for quiet games). We decided that it was time to regroup before going any further. This regrouping was quickly achieved and we ended up with:

Rules group — dealing with regulations and their publicity.

41

Areas group — to come up with a plan of the playground and where activities should be allowed.

Council group — to design a coherent approach to the council.

Make it happen

In the event, the children were surprised at how well their ideas were received and the extent to which change was achieved. We now have a divided playground and a lot more activity. I was really pleased to find that the children were reporting much less bullying going on. 'We're too busy to bully now', said Matthew, and I'm sure he had a point.

So what next?

They say that solving one problem often leads to another. Well, the council group had unexpected success with their approach. It seems that if we can find some of the money, the council will provide manpower to set up an adventure playground. So our next real problem is about to begin — fundraising for the adventure playground!

In one example it is possible to give only a flavour of the problem solving process. In particular, this example gives only a hint of the teacher's role. This is something we return to in some detail in Chapter 6; at this stage we would like to highlight just the flow of activity from class discussion at the beginning and end. After the 'P' and 'R' stages, the class formed a number of small groups and these worked fairly independently during the 'O', 'B' and 'L' stages. The class came together again for the 'E' stage and everyone was involved in the 'M' stage. Finally, children need a chance to look back over what has been achieved and to learn from failure as well as success. This is the all important 'S' stage.

PROBLEMS and problem solving

In the introduction to this book we said that we were interested in covering a wide range of problem solving activity, from puzzles to projects in fact. The PROBLEMS acronym suggests a simple way of bringing this range of activity under the one umbrella, as shown in the diagram opposite.

The smallest type of activity is the puzzle. Here the question is well formulated and the answer usually known. We shall refer to this as Level 1.

The next type of activity we call a mini-problem. Here the question to be answered needs to be formulated before work on a solution can begin. This is the hallmark of a Level 2 type of problem. It is often the case that the first attempt at finding a solution is unsatisfactory and the problem solver has to loop back to an earlier stage to perhaps redefine the question, collect different data or analyse the data differently.

The third type of activity, which we call Level 3,

is that of the full blown project or real problem. As in the case study, Playtime, the hallmark of these activities is the all important 'M' stage. Children are seldom given the chance to really make something

happen even though as a learning experience it is second to none.

In the diagram, we have left the 'S' stage out of each of the levels, as we feel that a review session is relevant no matter what the children are working at. Here is what Nicola wrote after the Playtime project.

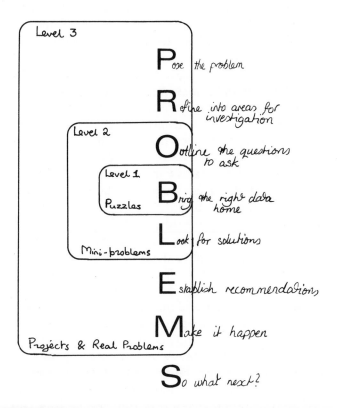

If I had to solve another problem I would firstly......

① Consult the class and ask for suggestions
② Accept some ideas and Reject some ideas.
③ Agree what had to be done, split up into groups.
④ Have a survey if necessary (You can't make decisions unless you ask everybody)
⑤ Make a plan.
⑥ Then do it

Nicola

How to use the PROBLEMS acronym

Perhaps the most important role of the PROBLEMS acronym is to serve as a guide for action in the classroom.

Level 1 — the 'B' stage only

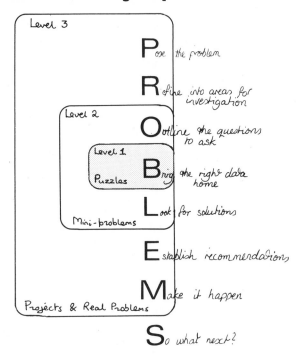

Level 3

Level 2

Level 1

Puzzles

Mini-problems

Projects & Real Problems

Pose the problem

Refine into areas for investigation

Outline the questions to ask

Bring the right data home

Look for solutions

Establish recommendations

Make it happen

So what next?

In Chapter 1, 'Ways In', we were careful to suggest that the starting point for problem solving was with puzzles. In Part 2 you will see that almost all the suggestions for problem solving start with an Introductory Activity. On the whole, these are pitched at the level of puzzles and, as such, encompass the 'B' stage of the PROBLEMS acronym. Our experience of working with children convinces us that it's best to start small and develop confidence before tackling more

ambitious projects. But there are other reasons for suggesting that the 'B' stage is a good starting point.

First, most pupils will be able to complete one of the Introductory Activities in a single lesson. This means that there is no need to disrupt the syllabus or timetable when problem solving activity is introduced. Classroom management too is made easier with the Introductory Activities as it is a fairly easy job for the teacher to make sure that the relevant materials are available for students to use. Even when a class has made progress and is beginning to take on more ambitious work, it is not a bad idea to return to a simpler activity. Amongst other things, this gives the children a chance to notice that they are making progress.

Starting with puzzles can give pupils the opportunity of swift success and a feeling of achievement. This is important in building confidence. And because the Introductory Activities can be approached at so many different levels, they give the pupils a chance to use the mathematics that they feel comfortable with. This too can boost confidence to have a go and try ideas out.

We have also found that these small problems serve as a valuable introduction to collaborative group work. Frequently a group can divide a task into parts that can easily be managed by individuals within a group. Particularly when there are a number of trials to be conducted or separate items of data to be collected, a group of children can experience the power of collaborative work when they learn to divide the task up and then collate their findings. The Introductory Activities, then, give the children a chance to develop an understanding of the ground rules of collaborative group work which then serves as an invaluable model for future work.

Even with work at this level, it is important to get children to explain their ideas. This will happen naturally as a part of working in a group but needs to be stage-managed by the teacher when it comes to making a report to the whole class. Because two groups will seldom have adopted exactly the same approach to a problem, there is often a fascinating cross-fertilisation of ideas that can result from report-back sessions. Most important is that children soon see the pay-off if they can listen and comment constructively when they hear about the approach that another group took to the problem they have been tackling.

Level 2 — the 'O', 'B' and 'L' stages

Following the Introductory Activities, we have usually been able to suggest a number of Extension Activities that children can tackle next. While some of these are fairly prescriptive, the aim is to suggest to children that they could start outlining their own questions. Indeed, many of the extensions have been developed by us using the simple technique of saying:

'What if I change this aspect of the problem?'

For instance, in Leap Frog the first extension is to ask what happens if you alter the number of counters. Another 'what if . . .' extension is to

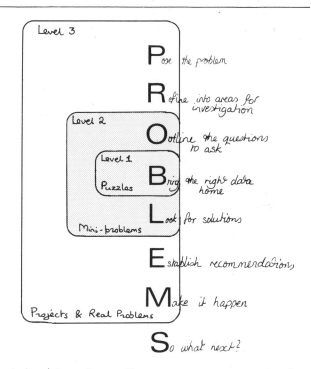

change the rules and leap over two counters rather than one. Going in a different direction you might increase the number of colours and have three sets of counters with the first and third having to change places, and the second ending up back in the middle. We hope that in time children will learn to generate their own questions from any given starting point.

The wider scope of problems that involve the 'O', 'B' and 'L' stages brings out the need for a group to agree on goals, set up hypotheses, decide on approaches and pick appropriate techniques.

45

Also, solutions may need to be validated — remember the first solution of the 'It's Boring' group and the reception it got from the rest of the class. Experience in explaining and convincing others and producing the necessary support for your arguments is an important part of the 'L' stage.

Also important to learn is that things won't always work out first time. It may be necessary to loop back and redo some work that has been unsatisfactory. The three main options for looping back in this way are:

• analyse the data differently,
• collect new data,
• change the question,

and each one takes you back to a different stage of the heuristic. This is shown on the following diagram.

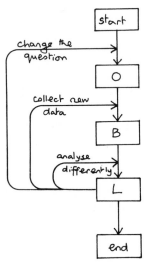

Level 3 — All stages of PROBLEMS

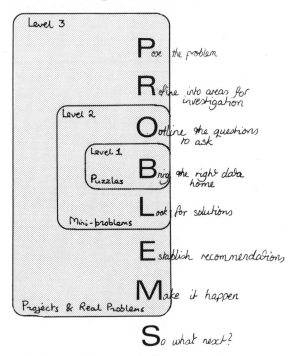

Whether the whole class is working on a real problem or a group of pupils has picked a project, an essential ingredient of tackling an extended activity is that it be something of genuine interest to them. We find it useful to think in terms of three kinds of activity:

• something to know,
• something to do,
• something to find out about,

and these headings can often serve as useful starting points for a class (or teacher) when looking for a promising real problem or project topic.

Initially, the scope of the activity, whether it be to organise a Christmas Party or exploring all the possibilities of a game like Leap Frog, will be too large for an individual to encompass. The problem needs to be clarified and then broken down into manageable parts. These steps are covered by the 'P' and 'R' stages of the PROBLEMS acronym. Then, after the 'O', 'B' and 'L' stages, the component solutions need to be assembled into a coherent whole and action needs to be taken. With a project, this usually means organising information and results to produce a comprehensive report, often with the arguments for and against clearly spelt out. With real problem solving the result should always be that something actually happens as a result of the work that has been done.

In order to sustain activities of this kind over a longish period (four weeks of regular involvement is quite common), the children need a real sense of purpose, to know that something will result from their efforts. The pay-off comes when the work is completed and children get a great sense of satisfaction that they themselves have made something happen. Along the way, they will have been planning and taking decisions, generally developing a sense of responsibility for their work. We mention this to bring out the contrast between Level 3 kinds of activity and the normal run of things in the maths classroom. It really does make sense to make a gradual transition between the two.

5 KNOWING HOW TO

- covering some of the key strategies that are needed by problem solvers.

In one classroom after another we have observed children having great difficulty both in organising their work and in describing or explaining their thinking and findings. As we reflected on what we saw happening, we began to think about what the children need in order to be able to carry out and record this type of work. The following key areas began to emerge:

• knowing how to get started

• knowing how to collect or generate various types of data

• knowing how to talk or write about their work and findings

and, particularly in project work,

• knowing what is expected of a good project.

At first glance, perhaps this is not a very impressive or daunting list. We hope to show how each of these areas represents quite a task for a busy teacher, and especially for teachers who feel that they are not trained to teach these skills There do seem to be a number of essential strategies that help children to know how to tackle the items listed above. Also, it does seem possible for children to learn these strategies ... as the next example shows.

A group of twelve-year-old pupils was working on the following Finger Exercise puzzle, and their report outlines the strategy they used.

Finger Exercise

Find a way of putting the digits 1–6 in these boxes so that the sum is correct.

STRAGETY

4 in group: we each chose a number in this box → ■□ and went through the whole possible outcomes

We worked out that a 0 or 5 cannot be possible in either □ ■ because

it will result in a 0 or 5 at the end. After 1 member of the group had finished all the possibilities in 4 (top left hand corner) she tried 5 and found that $54 \times 3 = 162$

You must work in some kind of pattern so that you are able to work systematically

J. Weston
J. Banham
O. Cane
R. Malin

Perhaps the first strategy that children learn is:

Look for a pattern.

Indeed, pattern searching is a common strategic thread through all kinds of learning, and as such is self-explanatory. In our experience, 'look for a pattern' is the strategy children adopt most naturally. When starting on a problem, this strategy is another way of trying to find an idea or hypothesis that can guide subsequent work. With pattern-searching as a goal, the task of collecting or generating data has a purpose to it. And at a later stage, looking for a pattern can involve formulating a general rule by which findings can be summarised and communicated to others. Thus 'look for a pattern' is a strategy that can be used at all stages of problem solving.

Knowing how to get started

With project work, we have all too often seen students become fired with enthusiasm about a topic, only to see this enthusiasm fizzle out at the first hurdle. It seems to us from various observations and discussions that we've had with children that the main reason is the hedonic rush which happens when a project is introduced. Rather than stop and think about what a project or problem involves, how and where information will be collected, and what the pros and cons are, the student's own views, opinions and preferences act as a 'need' to get going, often on a topic that is too ambitious, too broad or too limited.

Happily, there is a technique that can be used to slow down this initial phase and enable students to get a more realistic view of what is involved in their particular topic.

The choice of project is the first hurdle. Some students will just choose a topic that they think is easy, while others will choose one that really interests them. A worthwhile exercise is to ask each student to think about and explain:

• why they want to work on a particular project,

• why it interests them,

• what they think they'll learn from it,

• what they think is involved in it, and

• why they think they'll make a good job of it.

These are what we call advance organisers.

The advantages of advance organisers are that they make quite clear to the student at the outset whether they have an interesting project, as well as possibly highlighting some new ideas related to it. Having a sounding board in this way will also enable the students to clarify their own thinking about the project and how motivating it might be. It will also highlight right at the beginning any one-sided or rigid views that a student has that might hinder progress later on.

From one point of view, the problem Joining Triangles is a bad one because the result is surprisingly hard to find.

Joining Triangles

Using 5 triangles shaped like this:

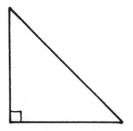

how many different shapes can you make?

But from another perspective it offers a valuable opportunity for children to try one of the important strategies in problem solving:

Try a simpler case.

If in doubt about how to get started on a puzzle or problem, it is often helpful to reduce the question to something more easily manageable. On the next page you can see how one group of eleven-year-olds used this strategy with 'Joining Triangles'. Initially this group was struggling to get into the problem as they found it very difficult to keep track of the many different patterns that five joined triangles make. Once they started to simplify, progress was possible. You can see examples of this group's work in the next column.

Knowing how to collect and generate data

As well as helping children to get off to a good start, the strategy of 'try a simpler case' is useful for generating information from which ideas about the problem can grow. It is similar to a second useful strategy which we call:

Be specific.

We will think about this strategy more in the context of project work, as this is where the scope of the topic often requires narrowing down before it can usefully be tackled.

The ability to collect or generate data is central to project work and problem solving. There is a tendency for students to copy great chunks from books. This is partly due to the fact that many of their reading and learning activities have been passive. They have not been expected to bring anything to activities or to do anything with what they've read, heard or seen. In problem solving work the reverse is what must happen.

Firstly, the child, not the teacher, must decide what information is required and what avenues of investigation must be followed. This is not so easy as it sounds. The first hindrance to making this decision is the vast scope of some of the very general projects or problems chosen. Examples of

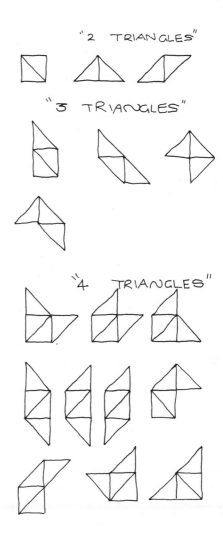

these that we've seen are 'games', 'sports' and photography'. The children working on these projects were fired with enthusiasm, yet quickly tired of their topics. Discussions with them soon revealed that their topics were so broad that they were daunted by the range of resources dealing with them. They didn't know where to start or how to organise the diverse information they were finding.

Discussion with David's group about their photography project took the form of questions aimed at getting them to talk about:

• what they already knew about photography;

• what they wanted to know;

• what they wanted to be able to do as a result of their project.

During this conference it transpired that David already knew a lot about photography and wanted to make an informed decision about which camera to have for his birthday. He wanted to join up with Eddie to be able to take photographs of planes as they took off and landed. The group's resulting project then was not about photography but about two much smaller fields:

1. how to find out which camera was best for this purpose;
2. how to take good photographs of aeroplanes.

Having refined the topic into two specific areas or subgoals, they soon realised that they needed to visit camera shops, collect brochures and try to talk to some photographers. They also needed to see what the features of a good flight photograph were, to find out about film speeds and where would be the best place to stand to take these photographs. The group was now able to make a plan of action, asking:

• What information do we need?

• Where could we find this information?

• When can we collect it?

• How can we collect it and approximately how long will it take?

In another situation, a group of boys wanted to prove that 'boys are better than girls'. They hadn't a clue where to begin other than by 'having a football match, boys v. girls': silly, of course, but they were unsure of how to proceed. A conference with this group focussed on questions about what better means, and better at what. They then realised that what they wanted to prove was that boys were actually cleverer than girls because, they said, they already knew that boys were stronger. They decided then that the data they wanted would not come from books but from experiments and the statistics that they could produce from them.

By moving from the general project headings to more specific ones, that is, from 'boys are better than girls' to 'boys are better than girls at general knowledge', the children were then ready to ask specific questions about what information they needed to collect, how to collect it and, equally importantly, what they were going to do with it when they had got it.

For the 'boys are better than girls at general knowledge' group, the problem was initially a major one of organisation. They wanted a Twenty Questions panel game, boys against girls. They wanted to do it for each grade level too to ensure that their sample was fair and representative. They also wanted to IQ test each class so that the teams were matched. Their first step was a plan of things to do before the tests and panel games. After many false starts without a plan, they set themselves to be systematic by:

• finding questions for each grade;

• setting an IQ test for each grade;

• finding out from other staff if they would agree to this;

• establishing rules and scoring for the panel game;

• trying it with their own class to see if it worked.

From then on, for this group it was plain sailing.

Having identified the types and sources of information needed, the task of gathering it can still be a problem. We observed one group responsible for making suggestions about where their class could go for a day trip. They had identified the following factors:

• it must be within 80 kms of school;

• it must be inexpensive;

• it must be able to cater for 32 children;

• it must occupy at least 3 hours;

• it must be interesting and enjoyable.

The group had no system or organisation. Each group member was doing his own thing, each brochure was being pored over by each group member, phone calls were being duplicated and when they came to put all their data together, there was much confusion. They had lots of scraps of paper with information on them but didn't know what to do with it.

What they really needed was help to share out the work load, not duplicate it, and a skills session on producing an attributes matrix was quickly held. We began this by asking the group to reformulate their factors into questions that could be asked about each place to visit. Using a large sheet of paper we then helped them to arrange their data as follows.

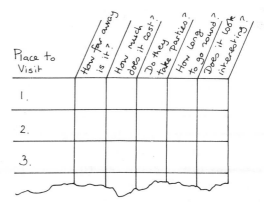

By report-back time they had their information sorted and were able to put the possible choices to the rest of the class.

This last example highlights a further strategy that is often useful, namely:

Find a good representation.

For a group we observed working on the Leap Frog problem, the problem of collating data on a good representation was very different.

Leap Frog

In the game of Leap Frog the aim is to swap the positions of two sets of counters. This is the starting position.

They rushed in and began playing with great enthusiasm, not recording anything. When one group member shouted, 'I've done it', the others wanted to know how. He couldn't remember and couldn't do it again. They soon realised that if they were going to try to find the smallest number of moves required or to establish a pattern for this puzzle, they must keep a record of their moves. After some struggling, they decided on the following format for their recording.

54

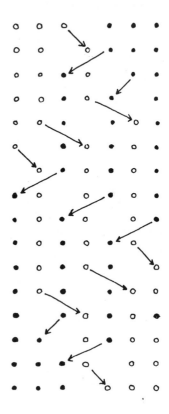

The resulting diagram caused a lot of excitement within this group because it showed that there was a kind of symmetry to the pattern, and also from it they hypothesized that the halfway move should always cross the mid-point.

Paul and Ranjit had been working on the introductory activity for the remainders problem:

Remainders

Find a number which, when divided by 3 leaves remainder 1 and when divided by 4 leaves remainder 2.

They had actually solved the problem and were preparing a way of interpreting their answer to explain to the rest of the class, when Ranjit hit on a really nice idea. He showed Paul how you could do it on a clock face.

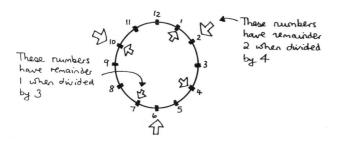

By showing their findings on the diagram, it was easy for them to explain their idea to the rest of the class. And, fortunately, they had stumbled on a representation that could be used for further work on the extension activities.

There are many occasions when finding a good representation is the key to finding the solution to the problem. But the representation on its own is seldom enough. As in the following example, it is **often essential to:**

Be systematic.

Here is the work of a group of thirteen-year-old children as they are solving the Three-Eighths problem.

Three-Eighths

In how many different ways can you shade three-eighths of a 2×4 rectangle using whole squares?

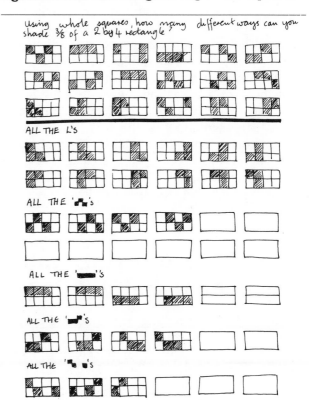

Look first at the work above the line. There are plenty of examples of shaded rectangles, but no systematic attempt was being made to list the possibilities. And this group of children was not alone. Their teacher had noticed that very few children in the class had any feeling for what it is like to adopt a systematic approach. She deliberately left the class to flounder with the problem for 10 minutes or so before they were called to order. She then suggested how a systematic approach might prove helpful. You can see the difference when you look below the line. What began as a disorganised collection of examples of three-eighth shadings suddenly changes into an organised set.

In the problem section there are quite a few examples where the systematic use of an appropriate representation is the key. All Change, MacMahon's Triangles, Magic N-grams and Spirolaterals are all particularly susceptible to this approach and could profitably form the basis of a problem solving session along the lines described above.

Knowing how to talk and write about their findings

When it comes to talking or writing about their findings, children are faced with many difficulties: knowing where to start, what to include and what to omit, how to structure it, and what language style to use being the major ones.

Knowing where to start, what to include and what to omit are problems for any writer, and more especially so after several hours' or even weeks' work on a problem. So many false starts and mistakes, so much data collected, so many hypotheses stated, tested, proved or abandoned, so many side-tracks, so much emotion, that it is almost impossible to sift through the jungle.

There are general questions that might guide this sifting process:

• Why did your group get started on this project?

• What excited your group or made you curious?

• What did your group want to find out about or do?

• What did your group find out or learn as a result of your work?

• Did your group make any mistakes?

• Which aspects does your group want to tell the class about?

Jottings made at this stage should indicate a starting point and make clear which information is superfluous.

Style and structure

The list of jottings made in answer to questions of the type just listed can then be classified either as

56

a topic web or as lists of related ideas. These might then indicate the sequence and the structure of the text. For example, the camera club group generated a list of features that they thought a camera should have. For them, a comparison structure was required, one which would enable them to describe and compare the cameras that were suitable for their purpose.

From the list of jottings that the 'Boys are better than girls' group generated, they decided that a suitable point to talk or write from would be a problem-solution structure. Their *problem* was how to set up the experiment to generate the data. Their *solution* as careful planning and the running of IQ tests and a Twenty Questions panel game. They were definitely not going to reveal the results!

Often the structure required will suggest a language style. At other times, however, the audience or purpose will determine how the argument should be phrased. If the report is for the class , a spoken or written narrative might be suitable. If, however, the report is to go to the town council (as did the report for the playtime project) to persuade them to or not to take a particular action, then the report needs to be more formal. For young children whose only print experience has been with narrative texts, a great deal of assistance will need to be given if they are to attempt formal or expository reporting. For older secondary students, however, who are used to expository language, some guidance will be needed if they are to write in the first person - another reason for ensuring that children hear and read lots of project reports and discuss the writing style.

Knowing what is expected of a good project

A major concern about project work is the often poor quality of the traditional project work folders presented by many children. These contain jumbled ideas, chunks copied from books and are usually deliberately stretched out with lots of pictures, etc. — hardly surprising really when you think about the degree of organisation required to present a project well. This organisation and related skills are seldom taught in schools. However, if problem solving and project work are to be successful, this aspect of the work needs to be given much thought. Here is how one (fictional) child was introduced to project work.

'Miss Beale said you would show me round, to look at the projects,' said Andrew.
'Why, do you want to copy one?' asked Victor, lifting a strand of hair and exposing one eye. 'You could copy mine, only someone might recognise it. I've done that three times already.'
'Whatever for?' said Andrew. 'Don't you get tired of it?'
Victor shook his head and his hair. 'That's only once a year. I did that two times at the junior school and now I'm doing that again,' he said. 'I

do fish every time. Fish are easy. They're all the same shape.'

'No, they're not,' said Andrew.

'They are when I do them,' said Victor. He spun his book round, with one finger, to show Andrew the drawings. His fish were not only all the same shape, they were all the same shape as slugs. Underneath each drawing was a printed heading: BRAEM: TENSH: CARP: STIKLBAK: SHARK. It was the only way of telling them apart. The shark and the bream were identical, except that the shark had a row of teeth like tank traps.

[from *Thunder and Lightnings* by Jan Mark]

These statements seem to suggest, then, that not only do the students not know what's expected of them but also that many teachers don't really know what a project is, or should look like. Nor, more importantly, do they fully value the effort that goes into presenting a project even if on the surface it looks like quite a poor one (e.g. how do you give credit for or even acknowledge the hours of grappling that goes into worrying about which topic to choose, which data to use and how to get started on the writing?). For most of us, even as adults, putting the first few marks on a piece of paper, deciding on the writing style, worrying about the content and its acceptability is still a daunting task, so why are we surprised that our students find this difficult?

So why are they so unprepared for project work? Firstly, we think, because they don't know what a project really is, or what a 'good' or 'bad' project looks like; nor do they know what the ground rules are or by what criteria their work will be assessed. The first task facing a teacher in order to introduce project work then is to make explicit to the students what is expected. There is no point saying to them that you want them to engage in a personal extended piece of work if it is then to be scrawled all over in red ink, criticised and given what seems like an arbitrary grade. As one twelve-year-old put it:

> You work for the whole term on a topic like writing a fantasy novel and really get into it, then you give it in, wait 3 months to get it back, only to see that the teacher doesn't think much of the ending. Charming!

If you show pupils projects that you feel are good or bad and explain why, they will get a feel for what is expected of them. The pupils can then read, assess and discuss some projects for themselves, in this way focussing on and highlighting what they think are the important qualities. Key issues in project work can then be discussed from a common ground and might focus on such aspects as:

• project content;

• originality of ideas presented on the approach to them;

• new knowledge gained about the subject;

• the way in which mathematics has been used to find or present results;

- the quality of explanation;

- coherence of ideas, argument, etc.;

- the quality and style of presentation.

In this way the teacher and students can negotiate quite clearly what the ground rules of project work are. By the end of such discussions the students should have grasped the idea that a project should be their work, not chunks from books, etc.; that it should contain their ideas and views and that they will be allowed to negotiate with the teacher to demonstrate the 'behind the scenes work and struggle' that went into producing it. They should also have established quite clearly the criteria for a successful project and how it will be assessed.

Since some sort of final assessment is almost certainly going to be made, why not encourage students to read, edit and discuss their projects at every stage with their peers, and possibly even assess each other's projects. After all, they are closely involved and probably more sensitive to the effort and pain that went into the production of a project than the teacher is.

6 THE TEACHER'S ROLE

– a key feature of problem solving is that the children should be in the driver's seat; this has important implications for the role of the teacher.

In much of what goes on in the maths classroom it is the teacher who plays the leading role. It is the teacher who tells the class what they will do. It is the teacher who decrees how it shall be done, and it is the teacher who decides when it's finished. Listen to the dialogue in such a lesson; it is the teacher who does most of the talking. The more the teacher talks, the less the pupils say. As the teacher's input gets longer, so the pupils' responses reduce, almost to 'Yes, no, three bags full'. It is the teacher doing all the thinking, asking questions to which there is already an expected right answer. Dishonesty creeps in here, as comments such as:

'Try again.'
'Have you left your thinking cap at home.'
'Now you're on the right lines.'

separate the so-called bright sparks from the less able, perpetuating the 'I'm no good at maths', 'I'm a failure' myths. This may seem a bit extreme but no doubt you get the point; all too often the teacher does play the role of central processor. The situation is set up by the teacher. The students are working well; working well, that is, until the teacher, trying to fulfil an expected role, intervenes with:

'Right, let's talk about what you are doing.'

The buzz stops, the students talk to the teacher, the teacher generates comments, questions or instructions constantly. The teacher is the mediator. The pupils cease talking to each other or looking at each other for confirmation of their ideas. Instead they fall back into role, expecting the teacher to know, to tell, to correct and to redirect them. This is, after all, what teachers are for ... or is it?

Should the teacher ask questions when what's really intended is to guess what's in the teacher's mind? Should the teacher direct all activity, leaving little initiative or need to think for the groups? Should the teacher, albeit unwittingly, disrupt the flow of a cohesive group? Should the teacher do most of the talking, and not the students? Should the teacher have the last say, judging the quality of the work, deciding when it's finished or unfinished? Finally, should the work satisfy the needs of the teacher or those of the student?

One thing that we would like to make clear, here and now, is that, much as we are about to suggest possible changes in the teacher's role, we don't intend to make a suggestion about teaching style. We are well aware that teachers have their own style, their own personality, their own vitality. It is these qualities that make it possible for teachers to teach with the commitment and effectiveness that they do.

When we first attempted to get teachers to try out problem solving and group work, we had not made this distinction between role and style. We were working closely with a group of teachers who had tried nothing of this type before. We had a few in-service sessions and also went into each classroom, in a sense demonstrating how we thought problem solving should be done.

We talked to the teachers as we have done in this book about problem solving and its organisation. In addition, however, we talked about the importance of asking open-ended questions and about how much teachers should talk, when they should bring the groups together and how they should get them reporting back. The teachers and pupils alike picked up our hidden curriculum as they watched us teach. They thought that we expected them to emulate our teaching style, and they tried valiantly to incorporate all our ideas into their first tentative attempts at problem solving. At a time, then, when they were already on shaky ground, lacking confidence in problem solving techniques and what to expect from them, these teachers were also trying to change their whole teaching style to bring it in line with what they thought we were expecting.

The eruption had to come. Explosively the teachers vented their frustrations at the third workshop we had with them. Judith finally encapsulated their feelings when she said:

'We feel taken over. We've lost our personalities. We do it and it works, but we don't fit in.'

Of course we were surprised to find that they felt they had to be like us or that they felt we'd tried to prescribe their teaching style. In retrospect though, we realised that that was exactly what we had done. At last the air was cleared and all agreed that they wanted to carry on problem solving ... but they wanted to do it their way. Very soon after this, as each of the teachers became confident and committed, their own styles and personalities in the classroom re-emerged. This restored equilibrium seemed to suit all concerned and for us at least made the point that teachers don't need to change their spots, only their stripes.

So just how does the teacher's role change in problem solving? First, there need to be some general changes. Rather than acting as central processor, imparting ideas etc., the teacher needs to be seen as a resource; someone who is available to talk with the students but not at them, and also someone who will enter in, share experiences with the students and all the while be available for whatever needs may arise, such as teaching a new technique if required, providing resources when asked or even clearing the way for students to take their problem solving outside the classroom if necessary.

More specifically there are three key roles that the teacher needs to adopt if the path to solutions is to be satisfactorily pursued. These are the roles of:

• creator

• facilitator

• intervener.

Each of these roles serves a different but vital purpose in problem solving. So let's look at the creator role first as this is the first role to come into play.

The creator role

The central aspect of this role, and perhaps the most important of all teacher roles, is that of setting an environment in which problem solving is possible, or to put it another way, the teacher needs to create an appropriate emotional climate. This may not be straightforward, especially if the students have had many years at school in teacher-directed activities, playing 'Guess what's in the teacher's mind', responding to questions to which the teacher already has a right answer in mind, or just following instructions.

The teacher's role here then is to create a safe, trusting, honest environment in which the pupils can develop an awareness of what their role is to be. It needs to be made explicit to the students that they are to be responsible for setting their own goals and criteria. An atmosphere is required in which every participant feels able to contribute ideas, however loosely formulated they may be and in which being creative or divergent is valued, even if some blind alleys are generated. Within this type of trusting environment it should be possible for the pupils to work at a level of complexity or completion with which they feel confident or satisfied. This means, for example, that the students may end up using the mathematics with which they feel comfortable rather than that which a teacher would expect.

Once this environment is created, the students should have a good understanding of what the ground rules are. Some of these rules will have to be made explicit and are essential to the students' understanding of what is expected of them. These ground rules would include the student knowing:

• what type of outcome is expected (e.g. report, model, etc.) and the type of presentation;

• that they are doing the thinking and making the decisions, i.e. that this is going to be their piece of work;

• that their ideas are important and valued;

• that they will choose the group they want to work in, choosing by interest rather than friendship;

• that this work is not just fun or a game, rather that it is an essential extension or complement to normal classwork, not different or separate from it;

• when an investigation or problem is finished to their satisfaction.

A key feature of problem solving and investigative work is the negotation process. If, as we hope, the student is going to do the thinking and make the decisions, opportunities for collaboration and negotiation are essential.

So what do we mean by negotiation? As an example, here is an account of the conversation held between one group of eleven-year-olds.

MARK: I think we should definitely have an animal corner.

GEOFFREY: What would you keep there and who'd look after them?

TINA: Yeah, who'd look after them in the holidays?

TRACEY: Well I think having animals is important.

GEOFFREY: Yes that's OK, but what about the plants if they get out or something?

MARK: We'd have to work out how much it'd cost to feed them and all.

WAYNE: Don't animals attract flies and things?

CHRISTINE: Listen, why don't we put it to the vote so that everybody gets a say?

Ideas are being offered, sometimes supported, at other times challenged, but the group is edging towards a shared goal. The students will need to negotiate their ideas in this way both with each other and occasionally with the teacher to ensure that they:

• don't have to work in isolation;

• can share, explore and clarify their ideas with a 'sounding board';

• can be reassured, have their ideas questioned and, if necessary, change the direction of their thinking.

Negotiation is essential at several stages of this type of work. Actually choosing and formulating a problem requires discussion with others about what will be involved and what the key factors are. This clarification and understanding should result

63

in a negotiated, agreed and clear understanding of the problem. Also, while formulating the problem, the students should negotiate the constraints on the goal and develop their own criteria for successful completion of the problem.

Prior to data collection or generation, the students again need to negotiate and discuss, to share ideas, explain their plans and justify the research methods to be used. Negotiation at these early stages is important to ensure that effort is not duplicated and that the areas of investigation are actually going to be useful.

When the data have been analysed and interpreted, the resulting solutions or recommendations should be presented and supported to convince others of the validity of the findings and results. This dialogue may, of course, highlight shortcomings in the findings and require the student to loop back and collect new data, interpret the data differently or find a new way of making a case.

The reflection process following the presentation also requires discussion about the degree of success of the solution or recommendation. The goals, constraints and criteria negotiated earlier can be used to determine the success of the work, to what extent the goals and constraints were met and how fully the criteria for success were satisfied. Discussion of 'mistakes' and 'successes' within the work can form the basis for discussion about how a problem might be handled differently next time.

In this way the students can develop confidence and perseverance. Having negotiated 'manageable' goals, i.e. chosen or formulated the problem at a mathematical level at which they feel confident, students can develop a feeling of success stage by stage, as well as at the end of the project. Providing an environment in which this negotiation can flourish is all part of the teacher's creator role.

The facilitator role

The teacher's role as facilitator includes all aspects of background work that will ensure smooth running of the project. This will include the organisation of the classroom to facilitate group work, the provision of resources required and behind-the-scene organisation for group, individual and class sessions as required.

Obviously students can't work in groups if they are sitting in rows. Nor can they make good use of resources if these aren't easily accessible. Resource provision requires some anticipation of needs and planning on the teacher's part. Either before introducing an investigation or after a problem has been formulated, the teacher needs to predict which resources might be required and to ensure that these or substitutes are available.

The behind-the-scene work includes such aspects as gaining permission for pupils to approach other pupils, teachers, the head, the caretaker, etc., as required. In some schools, if pupils are to move around in the corridors, indeed if they are to leave the classroom at all, permission has to be requested and people need to be forewarned that this is going to happen. Similarly, if the project is going to require phone calls to be made, permission needs to be obtained to enable the students to proceed uninterrupted or unhindered. These types of facilitation prevent a lot of frustration and disengagement with the problem. Imagine the frustration that a group who have worked hard and concentrated for a long time to prepare a plan of action must feel when, at their peak of activity, they are told that they are not allowed to use the phone ... or go to the supermarket for costings or whatever. For some, this type of refusal could result in such lack of belief that they are ever going to be able to do anything that the problem will be abandoned, and trust and motivation lost.

Another type of facilitator role is that of enabling the class to work individually, in groups or as a class. There are stages in problem solving when the class needs to work as a whole to enable them to formulate the problem, to take decisions, to fit recommendations together, to share some new skill or knowledge and also to reflect on the whole process. Initially, these whole class sessions need to be stage-managed by the teacher. At other times, you will see a need for the separate groups to report back either for negotiation, decision making or clarifying ideas. As the students gain confidence, they themselves will be able to say when they need a class report-back session.

When working with a class for the first time, we often found that a tight structure was needed to facilitate the students' activity. Before the lesson, we would choose two or three activities to offer to the class, and write these out on overhead projector transparencies. We would then use the following lesson structure as a guideline for our facilitating role.

1. Present problems on OHP and ask for discussions to ensure that the problems are understood. (5 mins.)

2. Ask each group to choose a problem, explain it in their own words and plan how to get started. (15 mins.)

3. Share explanations and plans, comment on and improve ideas. (10 mins.)

4. Complete work on chosen problem as far as possible. (20 mins.)

5. Report back by one member of each group, sharing of results. (10 mins.)

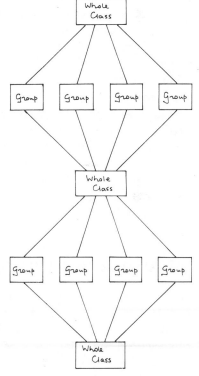

65

Facilitating group work also involves finding areas for the groups to actually work in. In some instances a group or groups might need to go off to work in different areas of the building. For example, one group may need to interview the kitchen staff about the food value of school meals, whilst another group goes off to investigate the range and cost of local takeaway foods, as happened on a 'School Dinners' problem once. This required facilitating by the teacher not only in terms of getting permission and arranging for the groups to do this, but also in planning insurance and supervision for the students leaving school premises.

Since not all phases of a real problem or project work come to an end at the same time, the teacher needs to ensure that groups still working on the problem can continue, whilst providing alternative activity for the groups who have finished. In some cases it is possible to redirect students to assist another group, but in other cases activity of a different kind has to be found for those not still busy on the problem.

The intervener role

One of the major differences in teaching during problem solving is that the teacher is free to be used as a resource and also has more time for observation and diagnosis of what the students are actually doing. These observations enable the teacher to develop an appropriate intervener role.

In many ways this is the most difficult task facing the teacher in problem solving work.

This difficulty arises because of the effect, both positive and negative, that an intervention can have for individuals, groups or the whole class. Decisions about if or when to intervene can be very difficult to make. These difficulties can then be further compounded by trying to decide what kind of intervention to make.

These decisions are compounded because the whole learning process and course of the solution can be altered or even destroyed by the wrong intervention, particularly by taking the problem away from the students, i.e. telling them what you would do next, or giving too specific a hint as Johnny did once.

Imagine the dilemma that Mr. Hamilton found himself in when his class was working on the design and construction of a puppet theatre. One group had responsibility for designing the main structure of the theatre which was to hold four children at a time.

Having brainstormed their area of the project, the design group very sensibly decided that what they needed was data about heights and widths of their class:

Because then we'll know how big to make the theatre. You know, how wide it needs to be and how tall and all that ... and um ... um ... where to put the whole thing ... um ... where the puppets ... oh yes ... the stage thing!

The data were collected and the group found the

width of everybody in the class, as shown below.

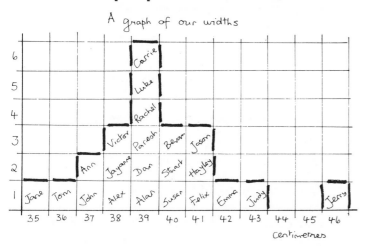

So far, so good, but then the students decided that the theatre should be as wide as the four widest children in the class plus some room for movement. By now, Mr. Hamilton was a little anxious; his first thought,

'Where are we going to put something that wide?'

was only just held back. Armed with heights and widths, the children were ready, or so they thought, to start construction. Knowing he couldn't let them waste valuable materials, let alone time, Mr. Hamilton intervened.

'Where are we going to fit this thing?'

The children were unperturbed and felt that, with a little rearranging, the classroom could accommodate it. The last thing he wanted to do was to take the problem away from the children by saying

'You can't make it that wide, it'll look silly.'

and yet he knew that their proposed size and shape would look very strange. So far the children had asked the question:

'How wide does it need to be to fit four children standing side by side?'

and, as shown below, had proceeded very well. They had:

1. outlined the question to ask	how wide to fit 4 children standing side by side?
2. brought the right data home	collected the data on each child in the class
3. looked for a solution	analysed their data to produce the answer —184 cms

After much thought about how to intervene, Mr. Hamilton said he thought that it would be best if the group drew a plan of their puppet theatre to scale so that they would know exactly how much wood, etc., they would need.

The group agreed that this was a good idea and set to. When they saw from their scale plan what

67

shape the puppet theatre was going to be (i.e. too wide for its height), they realised that something was wrong. For a short while they looked quite down at the mouth and frustrated. Jason asked:

'Does it have to be the four widest children?'
'Ah! No, it could be one wide one and three others.'

came the reply. Mr. Hamilton looked on, knowing that this still would be too wide, but he decided to let the group find that out for themselves. Eventually, the group decided that they had collected the wrong data. What they really needed to know, they decided, was the widths of all the children standing sideways. With renewed enthusiasm, they collected and analysed new data and still didn't get a manageable width.

Mr. Hamilton decided that it was time to offer direct assistance. His intervention was still in the form of a question,

'Do the children inside the puppet theatre have to stand in a line?'

He left the group with it, but the question was very much to the point. They were soon struggling to find alternatives to the straight line and were becoming quite argumentative when Jerry suggested:

'We could have two low down in front and two standing behind.'

Breakthrough! New measurements were taken and a suitable shape for the theatre decided upon.

In this particular example, the teacher was having to make important decisions about:

• whether to let the group pursue a 'blind alley';

• whether a 'failure' at this point would be too frustrating and detrimental to the problem solving process;

• whether to intervene and risk taking the problem away from the students;

• when and how to intervene.

Of course, he could have just told the group that what they were trying wouldn't work and he could have told them what would work. But what would the students have experienced or gained from that? At least this way they tried and failed. They thought about why they'd failed and persevered only to fail a second time, but then finally, with the help of direct assistance, they found a solution that would work. They felt elated, pleased with themselves, glad that they had struggled and, most important of all, they knew that it was their solution. They had thought of it.

By using questions, Mr. Hamilton had been able to redirect their thinking without telling the group what to try next. The thinking and decision making process was still required of the students; the teacher hadn't done it all.

In the intervener role, the teacher's questions are not yes/no questions nor are they 'guess what's in the teacher's mind' questions. Rather they are questions designed to try to unstick a stuck group without being too directive. They are designed to open up new avenues for students to explore, new courses of action for them to try.

A typical sort of intervention designed to help a group of students who are unable to generate ideas about their problem area is to encourage them to observe the situation. An example of this occurred when one class decided that they wanted to keep the school library tidy. They thought they needed some library rules but couldn't think what sort of rules were needed. Their teacher intervened and suggested that they might observe what happened in the library and see if they could find out how it got so untidy. After two or three observation sessions the group had found out why the library was so messy and were able to generate ideas for reorganising the shelves to make it easier to find and replace books, as well as producing rules for keeping the library tidy. When their rules and new system were put into action, they were delighted to find that it worked.

Skill sessions

When students are working on investigations and problems, it is possible for the teacher to observe what maths they are using confidently, what maths they are struggling with and where any difficulties are arising. Occasionally, the students will find themselves in a position where they need some maths that they have not yet learned about. In each of these instances, there are decisions for the teacher to make.

You need to consider whether the task is too complex for the student, in which case some help must be given. If the task is almost within range of the students and the students are motivated and task directed, it might be best to leave them to struggle. If you have foreseen that a new skill is required, questions about when to intervene arise. Decisions about whether to teach the skill before it's needed (in anticipation of it) or at the time it's needed (when motivation is high, but frustration may be imminent) need to be taken.

In one classroom a group of children had taken on responsibility for getting the best mix of soil for the courtyard garden that the class was making. The advice given in the catalogue was that sand, peat and gravel should be mixed in the ratio 2:3:1.

'What does that mean?'

they asked us. We then had to choose between telling them the answer and introducing them to the concept of ratio and its notation. We chose the latter and had a skill session on ratio that took them far enough to be able to work out their own ratio problem for themselves.

This then was a skill session held at the time the skill was needed. In earlier work with that class, we had seen ahead of time that the children would need to be able to work out the area of the irregular-shaped pond that was to be the centre-piece of the courtyard. This led to a skill session on estimating areas by counting half-squares and over that we conducted before the skill was needed.

Unfortunately, we cannot offer definitive advice

about when to hold a skill session; these decisions need to be based on the intuition and knowledge that a teacher has of a particular group, of how involved they are with the task, of how easily they become frustrated and give in.

In short, then, if investigations and problem solving are to become a part of school work, the teacher needs to be honest and sensitive to the needs of the children and to their individual strengths and weaknesses, experiences and attitudes. A key feature of this is the changing role of the teacher. The students will feel sufficiently secure to experiment and generate ideas in an atmosphere where the teacher is perceived as a trusted friend rather than as a figure of supreme authority.

ASSESSMENT 7

—looks at ways of evaluating children's development in the stages, strategies and skills of problem solving.

Every time we work with teachers on problem solving, they ask the same question:

'If children are working in groups, how will we assess what they are doing?'

No doubt similar questions have occurred to you too. Our reply is two-pronged. Firstly, once the children are involved in a problem the teacher is, in the traditional sense, redundant. That is, you are freed from the normal questions, such as

'What shall I do now, Miss?'
'Is this okay, Miss?'
'I don't understand what this means.'

You can actually spend time observing and listening to the children. Secondly, if children are choosing which problems they want to work on, or how they want to attack a problem and why, they will be setting their own goals. If they have set their own goals, then they will know when they've achieved them satisfactorily and won't need teacher approval to tell them so.

In this chapter we will be looking at what assessment is possible and appropriate in problem solving, and we hope to suggest general methods that can be used. The three areas that we will discuss are the assessment of:

• *stages* — focussing on the PROBLEMS model as a framework for assessment;

• *strategies* — covering the extent to which children show ability with the strategies described in Chapter 5, and

• *skills* — in which we relate problem solving work to the regular maths curriculum.

We also want to stress that the aim of assessment of problem solving is to look at the processes which the children use, much more than at the product of their efforts. Ticks and crosses are definitely not the order of the day.

Assessment of the stages

Since the key feature of problem solving is that the children are setting their own goals and taking their own decisions, they are in the best position for knowing to what extent they have satisfied those goals. The teacher's role is to encourage children and to provide opportunities for them, either orally or in the written mode, and to report on their progress. Use of student record books is a method of doing this that we have found very successful. After one or two attempts and discussions, the children have used record books to provide very detailed and useful information about their understandings and development with problem solving. On pages 73-5 we have given an example of a student record book that is designed to encourage individuals to keep a log of their progress through a short problem. If it does nothing else, the record book helps the pupils to see how important it is that they share ideas and results.

We have found that, after a few problem solving sessions, the process of keeping records serves other equally valuable functions. First, the process of keeping records of this type helps the pupils to look back over what has been achieved and how

they have developed. Next, they begin to compare their statements of intent (box 4) with aspirations when faced with a new problem (box 1). Then there is much to be gained from reflecting on whether the plan of action (box 2) was actually carried out, and if not, why not.

At first glance, you might think that page 3, *Gathering Information*, is rather superfluous, but our experience has been that it serves as a useful checklist for younger pupils and one that they feel able to expand upon when new skills are mastered. The lists also provide the impetus to think about what techniques might be appropriate to a particular problem. This can be important when problem solving sessions are first introduced as the pupils' expectation is that the current problem must be solved by either the topic of the previous lesson or by the method applied to the previous problem.

So, from the pupils' point of view, the student record book can play an important part in helping them to chart their development. And, of course, it can be equally useful for the teacher.

Even though collaboration in the task of solving the problem might obscure the development of an individual, the record books indicate this clearly. For some pupils, it might be that their growth shows itself in terms of attitude (box 1), while for others, the ability to comprehend and reproduce even another's attempt at a solution is often a considerable achievement. Also, the record books will give a picture of how well the pupils are learning to adopt a coherent approach to tasks in their problem solving activity. Initially, they will find this hard, but later they will be able to understand and reflect on their activity in terms of the stages of PROBLEMS. One headmaster friend found that his eleven-year-olds worked best when he shared the PROBLEMS acronym with them. In a fascinating report-back of their work on organising a Youth Club, the children used the acronym as a natural part of their dialogue.

'You remember when we were ready to bring the right data home?'
'We had a problem when we tried to look for solutions'

and so on. From an assessment point of view, these children displayed a remarkable ability to adopt a systematic approach to problem solving.

Problem Solving
Student Record Book

Name _____

Class _____

Problem Title _____

Page 1

73

1 Choosing the problem

This is the problem that my group wants to work on.

My reasons for choosing this problem are:

2 My plan of action

This list shows the things that I need to do and the order in which I will do them.

Gathering information

Here are some ideas about how you might gather information

try some examples
make some measurements
do a survey
make a scale drawing
look in a book.

Here are some ideas about how to use your information

look for a pattern
do some calculations
work out a formula
draw a graph
find an average
use percentages
make a chart or table.

Write down everything you do and keep it in this Record Book.

³ Sharing the findings

> These are some of the interesting and important things that we have found.

⁴ Next time

> The next time I do a problem I will do these things differently.

page 4

Assessment of Strategies

Jeffy, an eight-year-old learning disabled boy, provides an example of strategic thinking. He had been struggling with the simplest Magic N-grams problem.

Magic N-grams

Find out how to place the numbers 1, 2, 3, 4, 5, 6, 7, 8, 9 on this triangle so that the sum of the numbers on each side is the same.

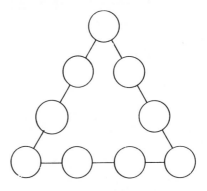

By trial and error he had made a start on finding out how the numbers 1—9 could be fitted on to the triangle so that all the sides would have the same total. His was not a difficulty with addition but with planning his work. His early attempts involved just randomly placing the numbered counters and then saying,

'Yes, it works' or 'No, it doesn't work'.

One comment,

'It won't work if the big numbers are in the corner'

set him to ask

'Will it work if the small numbers are in the corner?'

With a bit of help, he made his plan. Here it is, as he verbalised it with a little help from his teacher:

1. Try the small numbers in the corner.
2. Put one middle-sized number on each side.
3. Add it up — will it work?
4. Rearrange the middle-sized numbers till there's only a difference of one between the first two sides.
5. Now arrange the big numbers so they add up.

Success! He then was able to adapt his plan to try the middle-sized numbers and later the large-sized numbers in the corners. For him, this was just the beginning. He knew he'd been successful and now wanted to apply his rule to the smaller triangle to see if it worked there too.

From an assessment point of view, then, what can be said about Jeffy's attainment with strategic thinking? Comments like:

• starts with trial and error, probably an old trusted friend;

• able to see the need for a plan, but his first plan is based on intuition more than anything else;

• shows evidence of being systematic when guided by the teacher;

• able to carry out the plan and had success with it;

• goes on to apply the plan to a different context,

are all descriptive of what Jeffy did from a strategic point of view, and (please note) focus on what Jeffy could do rather than on what he couldn't.

It has been suggested that all children's activity is based on some sort of 'reason' or plan, and it is certainly our experience that this is true . . . although actually identifying the strategy can be difficult at times! However, as one becomes accustomed to looking at children's work in problem solving, it becomes easier to spot strategic thinking. In particular, one can notice various levels at which strategies are being used. For example, when Ann was involved in a research project to find ways of grading problem solving work, she used the following problem to highlight these levels.

Finger Exercise

Find a way of putting the digits 1–6 in these boxes so that the sum is correct.

After working through many pieces of written work, Ann was able to isolate six strategic levels for this problem as follows:

Strategic Level	Summary of Pupils' Work
1.	No system in evidence.
2.	Blockbuster approach with every possibility tried.
3.	Group work, sharing out of numbers.
4a.	Random sum to start, with numbers altered accordingly (up or down).
4b.	Rules generated such as can't multiply by 1 or 5 in units column.
5.	Either 4a or 4b, and keeping track of numbers efficiently.
6.	5 + coherent explanation.

On the next few pages we have reproduced examples of pupils' work at each of these levels. As you look through the examples, you will notice the gradual increase in sophistication. Of course, it would be a daunting task for individual teachers to attempt to produce such a classification for each problem presented to their class, but Ann found that many other problems could be analysed in a manner similar to that given above. From 'no system in evidence' through to 'strategy applied with

Problems   1,2,3,4,5,6   Aunas Vellan

$$^{1}64 \times 3 = 192 \qquad ^{3}36 \times 5 = 180 \qquad ^{1}65 \times 2 = 130 \qquad 62 \times 3 = 186 \qquad ^{1}52 \times 6 = 318$$

$$61 \times 4 = 244 \qquad 61 \times 3 = 183 \qquad ^{2}59 \times 3 = 177 \qquad ^{1}56 \times 3 = 168 \qquad 66 \times 3 = 198$$

$$34 \times 2 = 68 \qquad ^{1}46 \times 3 = 138 \qquad ^{3}26 \times 6 = 156 \qquad 52 \times 4 = 208 \qquad 51 \times 6 = 306$$

$$8{/}15 \times 6 = 90 \qquad ^{2}64 \times 5 = 320 \qquad ^{1}64 \times 3 = 192 \qquad ^{1}63 \times 5 = 315 \qquad ^{1}63 \times 6 = 378$$

$$^{2}56 \times 4 = 224 \qquad ^{1}56 \times 3 = 168 \qquad ^{5}53 \times 4 = 212 \qquad ^{2}65 \times 4 = 260$$

$$^{1}56 \times 2 = 112 \qquad ^{1}56 \times 3 = 168 \qquad ^{2}54 \times 6 = 324 \qquad ^{1}54 \times 3 = 162$$

$$^{3}56 \times 6 = 336 \qquad ^{3}56 \times 5 = 280 \qquad 52 \times 4 = 208 \qquad ^{1}53 \times 4 = 212$$

1. No system in evidence

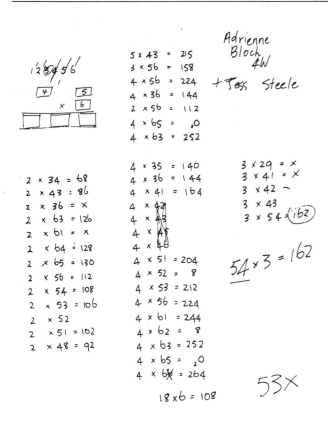

Adrienne
Bloch
4W

+ Jess Steele

$5 \times 43 = 215$
$3 \times 56 = 158$
$4 \times 56 = 224$
$4 \times 36 = 144$
$2 \times 56 = 112$
$4 \times 65 = {}_20$
$4 \times 63 = 252$

$2 \times 34 = 68$
$2 \times 43 = 86$
$2 \times 36 = \times$
$2 \times 63 = 126$
$2 \times 61 = \times$
$2 \times 64 = 128$
$2 \times 65 = 130$
$2 \times 56 = 112$
$2 \times 54 = 108$
$2 \times 53 = 106$
2×52
$2 \times 51 = 102$
$2 \times 48 = 92$

$4 \times 35 = 140$
$4 \times 36 = 144$
$4 \times 41 = 164$
4×42
4×43
4×45
4×46
$4 \times 51 = 204$
$4 \times 52 = 8$
$4 \times 53 = 212$
$4 \times 56 = 224$
$4 \times 61 = 244$
$4 \times 62 = 8$
$4 \times 63 = 252$
$4 \times 65 = {}_20$
$4 \times 6 = 264$

$18 \times 6 = 108$

$3 \times 29 = \times$
$3 \times 41 = \times$
$3 \times 42 \sim$
3×43
$3 \times 54 = 162$

$54 \times 3 = 162$

$53 \times$

We tested each no. by trial and error until we reached
$3 \times 54 = 162$

2. The blockbuster approach

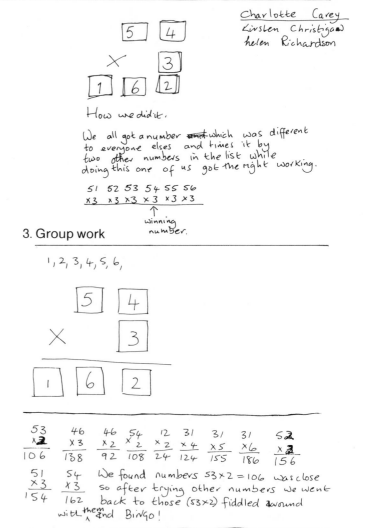

Charlotte Carey
Kirsten Christigan
Helen Richardson

How we did it.

We all got a number which was different to everyone elses and times it by two other numbers in the list while doing this one of us got the right working.

51 52 53 54 55 56
×3 ×3 ×3 ×3 ×3 ×3
          ↑
       winning
       number.

3. Group work

1, 2, 3, 4, 5, 6,

53	46	46	54	12	31	31	31	52
×2	×3	×2	×2	×2	×4	×5	×6	×3
106	138	92	108	24	124	155	186	156

51   54
×3   ×3
154   162

We found numbers 53×2 = 106 was close so after trying other numbers we went back to those (53×2) fiddled around with them and Bingo!

4a. Starting number altered

78

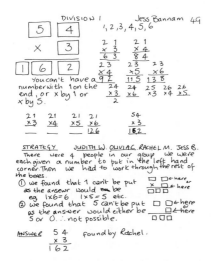

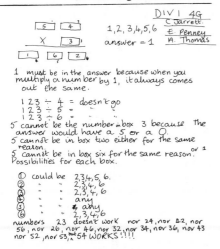

4b. Rules generated

1 must be in the answer because when you multiply a number by 1, it always comes out the same.

123 ÷ 4 = doesn't go
123 ÷ 5 =
123 ÷ 6 =

5 cannot be the number in box 3 because The answer would have a 5 or a 0.
5 cannot be in box two either for the same reason.
5 cannot be in box six for the same reason. or 1
Possibilities for each box.

① could be   234,5.6.
②   "   2,3,4,6
③   "   2,3,4, 6
④   "   any
⑤   "   any
⑥   "   2,3,4,6

numbers 23 doesn't work nor 24, nor 42, nor 56, nor 26, nor 32, nor 34, nor 36, nor 43 nor 52, nor 53, but 54 WORKS!!!!

5. Keeping track of numbers efficiently

Eleanor P. Margolies   Catriona Holland   SarahShewan

We began by eliminating numbers which were impossible in certain positions. When we knew that these could not be a '1' in   A B   we knew that therefore there must or   x C
be a '1' in the answer

Then working as a team we each chose a unit of ten for example Sam Catriona worked out all the possible combinations of 52-54 multiplied by 8 numbers 2-6 without a calculator. We discovered the answer this way.
Through elimination we already knew that the answer contained the figures 6 and 1 and that neither the original number or the multiple was 1

54
x 3 This is the answer!
162

6. A coherent explanation

coherent explanation', there seem to be reasonably distinct categories into which the children's work will fall. Also, the fact that this analysis can be done should be taken as justification that first, it is possible to assess the problem solving strategies, and second, such an assessment can be usefully couched in terms of a gradual development. We are not so sure, however, that marks are appropriate here as we can't really find any justification for adding (or averaging) strategic levels from one problem solving session to the next. A child who is getting the hang of 'Try a simpler case' may still find it difficult to 'Be systematic'. We find it more appropriate to think in terms of a profile. Once you have decided which strategies of problem solving are of concern to you, it is possible to record the pupils' development on a chart such as:

Strategy	no evidence	met but not used	used shakily	used	used confidently
Try a simpler case					
Be specific					
Be systematic					
Find a good representation					
Look for a pattern					

Level of attainment

The chart can be built up gradually. Each problem solving activity that you observe can be added to the chart, using an identifying number for the problem in the appropriate cell of the matrix.

The developmental record that the chart will show can be supplemented by the occasional check on how the pupils themselves feel they are progressing. For instance, you could ask them to rate themselves on the following statements.

1. When working on a problem, I know how to look for a pattern.

   CAN   6   5   4   3   2   1   CANNOT

2. If a problem is too difficult, I know how to try a simpler case.

   CAN   6   5   4   3   2   1   CANNOT

3. If a problem is too general, I know how to make it more specific.

   CAN   6   5   4   3   2   1   CANNOT

4. If I have got to collect or generate a lot of data, I can be systematic.

   CAN   6   5   4   3   2   1   CANNOT

5. I can use these diagrams to help me sort out information.

   List:

It is then interesting to compare your assessment with what the children themselves feel. It's fine when the two tally with each other, but a mismatch can be equally revealing, for both teacher and pupil. More often than not, a mismatch occurs because pupils are highly critical of themselves and actually rate themselves lower than they should. Alternatively, a mismatch can result from pupils being able to carry out a process without understanding the label attached to it. This might well reflect a lack of confidence in problem solving work.

Assessment of Skills

When we began working with teachers on problem solving we were as anxious as they were to ensure that mathematical skills were not neglected. Our first approach was to keep a regular check on the formal aspects of maths by completing a grid which listed skills across the top and pupils down the side.

The skills list was worked out to cover the teacher's syllabus and entries in the matrix were usually:

- ticks to indicate adequate competence,

- crosses to suggest that more work was needed

although some teachers preferred a more complex record, using up to four indicators in the cells of the matrix.

While this information was useful evidence that maths was actually taking place in problem solving sessions, we found that, when confronted with the need or opportunity to do maths, children often show more about their understanding and level of competence than ever seems to happen in formal contexts. We say this because in our experience we have found that it is not really accurate enough to say that a particular aspect of maths has been covered. Only when a child has shown evidence of knowing:

- when to do a sum;

- how to do the sum;

- how to make sense of the answer,

can one be sure that a given aspect has become part of the child's mathematical repertoire. In the Introduction to Part 1, we discussed the many approaches that just one class of students took to the Bag of Sticks problem. If you look back to page 8 you will see how revealing the work was about the pupils' understanding of triangles. Here is another example of this.

Francine, a low ability fifteen-year-old, hated mathematics lessons and usually misbehaved and disrupted those sitting near her. On our second visit to this particular classroom, we set Francine's group to work on the Three-Eighths problem.

Three-Eighths

In how many different ways can you shade three-eighths of a 2×4 rectangle, using whole squares?

There had been a lot of fuss before the group settled down and then, surprisingly, they began to work. Twenty-five minutes into the lesson, Francine shrieked. We dashed across to her as she was now waving her arm frantically in the air. She was excitedly shouting,

'I've got it. I've got it. I've solved this problem ... it's easy when you know how'.

She then explained to us her 'solution'. She had discovered that if half squares were shaded it would take six half squares to be the same as three whole squares. For the first time in ten years of schooling, Francine realised what fractions were and that 3/8 and 6/16 were, in fact, equivalent. The teacher looked baffled and obviously wanted Francine to continue with the set task. For Francine, however, the problem was over and she now needed to consolidate her discovery and try it with other fractions.

For us, the important lesson of this example was that problem solving can provide evidence of a pupil's level of understanding in a way that no other method of assessment can. But it takes patience and an open (rather than expectant) frame of mind to be alert to the information that problem solving can provide.

The teacher's role in assessment

We have stressed in Chapter 6 that the key teacher roles are creator, facilitator and intervener; perhaps we should add to that list the role of observer, as it is through observation of pupils engaging in problem solving work that so much about them can be learnt. One thing that the teacher can't do, when children are working collaboratively in groups, is to give each child a page of ticks and crosses and a score. And yet, the teacher is still accountable. The teacher has got to know what each child is contributing to a group, learning in the group and which strategies and skills are being used or developed.

To do this, refined skills of observation, listening (really listening) to what the children are saying and encouraging open discussion need to be developed. Only then will it be possible to make informed judgements about what children can do, both in terms of the maths skills that they use and the level of maturity they have reached in using the stages and strategies of problem solving.

Observations, to be useful, need to be objective because they form the basis of diagnostic and planning decisions. Objectivity can be achieved by establishing a clear and specific purpose or focus for observing rather than a vague and general purpose. From such specific observation, descriptive, constructive comments, rather than general lists of strengths and weaknesses can be made. A key feature of useful observations is that they focus on what the pupils do know, are learning and doing, rather than on what at first glance they seem to be learning or doing.

Before beginning an observation, the following pointers can prove helpful in ensuring a realistic and clear focus for observing.

1. Decide what to observe and why. Questions that help here are:
   • What do I want to assess — skills, processes, etc.?
   • What activity will ensure I get the type of evidence that I need?
   • Who will I assess — a group or individual?
   • How will this help me?
2. Consider the needs, concerns, feelings, attitudes, expectations and abilities of the group or individual.
3. Decide on the data to collect — dialogue action, product, manipulative skills, etc.
4. Decide on a recording method appropriate to the above — audio cassette, constant observation, observation at intervals, graphical representation of brief notes.

Immediately after making the observations, expand them, adding items of an anecdotal nature as well as accompanying examples of the pupils' work.

The information gained in this way is essential, not only so that a record or profile of each child's progress can be made, but also for diagnostic purposes. By using detailed observation, a teacher can consider any problems identified and plan what to do about them on the basis of objective information.

Pupil-teacher discussions

Observations alone will not provide all the information that a teacher needs. Discussions with the pupils will reveal a great deal of vital data. By discussion we have in mind a particular kind of dialogue where the children see the teacher as a trusted friend, where they know they can express their doubts and frustrations, their excitements and successes in an atmosphere of non-judgemental sharing.

This sounds easier than it is. And it won't necessarily happen overnight. There are subtle changes in the teacher's role that first need to be made. These changes revolve around the concept of teachers really getting to know their pupils, their interests and degrees of confidence. To do this, one has to listen with real interest to what the children have to say. Important features of these discussions are that:

• the teacher values the contributions that the children think are appropriate;

• the children, not the teacher, will be doing most of the talking;

• the teacher will be building on the comments of the children;

• the teacher will not be correcting errors;

• the teacher will allow short periods of silence for the children to safely formulate their thinking and ideas.

Openers to this kind of dialogue could be as simple as

'How's it going?'
'Your group's looking a bit fed up!'
'That was a tricky problem your group had with . . . How on earth did you overcome that?'

Just let the flood gates open and don't jump in too soon. Good luck to you and your class!

PART

2
THE PROBLEMS

INTRODUCTION

— a brief look at how Part 2 is organised, how to use the problems in the classroom and how to add to the list.

By now, many of the problems in this part of the book need little introduction; they should be good friends. But we think you may find it helpful if we say how the problems are organised, how we envisage their use in the classroom and how the problems can be added to.

After using some of the ideas in Part 2 directly, that is, lifting them straight off the page, we hope that you will be able to feel confident to freely adapt our suggestions to your own needs. Also, let's not forget that in every classroom there are some thirty or so willing collaborators in the teaching and learning process. Their ideas can, and should, become a major resource for problem solving work. Indeed, having expected that children would pose themselves trivial problems, we found this was far from the case. Instead, children take delight in asking particularly daunting questions and seldom give up on questions that they themselves have posed.

Organisation of the problems

Each problem is headed by an Introductory Activity. These activities are often, although not always, of a closed nature and intended to be so. The aims of the Introductory Activities are:

• to give a taste of a field of investigation that can be tackled later;

• to offer reasonable chances of success;

• to encompass, at most, a double period;

- to cover the full range of strategic thinking and mathematical skills;

- to be amenable to solution at a number of different levels.

Obviously, none of the Introductory Activities will cover all these aims, but, taken together, the problems are of sufficient variety and sophistication that there should be plenty to cater for all tastes.

The Extension Activities are rather different. When you start with an idea for a problem, it can always be changed this way or that to lead off in different directions. Sometimes the context can be altered. So, for example, the Best Buy idea can be applied to any product that interests the children . . . such as sweets.

Then it is often possible to make the problem more complex by adding more dimensions or increasing the number of variables. In the bibliography we have included a book that is devoted entirely to this idea, *The Art of Problem Posing* by Stephen Brown and Marion Walter. When children come to expect that a problem can be followed up by extension activities of the kind that we suggest, they will gradually begin to see ways of extending their own work into avenues that they themselves determine. Nowhere is this more true than in real problem solving. Our favourite tale here is of the class that planned an afternoon outing to their local town. This was soon followed by a day-trip to London and the class was last heard of planning an excursion to France.

But let's not lose sight of the following maxim:

Start Small.

A confined activity with an excellent chance of success can lead on to grander designs, but an over-ambitious goal in the early stages will often lead to nothing happening at all.

Using the problems in the classroom

After a decade of classroom reform in the sixties, the painful lesson was learnt that no material is teacher-proof. Well, this book isn't intended to be teacher-proof; quite the reverse in fact. All we can offer are suggestions and examples; from now on it's up to you. In particular you now have to decide:

- which problems to use with your class and when to use them;

- how to introduce the problems to the pupils (remember Chapter 1);

- in what way to use the extension activities;

- how much time you will set aside for problem solving work;

- how detailed will be the records that you keep.

At the same time, you will probably find that you are doing things in a slightly different way from the normal maths lesson. Expect this change to be gradual, both for you and your pupils.

Adding to the problems

We hope very much that you will want to make the selection of problems in Part 2 grow. First, there will be areas of maths that you want to cover for which we have made inadequate provision. Second, your own interests in this area may not be covered adequately. Third, new problems will arise from work that the children do and which you come across both in books and in your everyday life.

In any way that you can, let this section of the book become a starting point for the future.

THE PROBLEMS

All Change

Introductory Activity
Continue this sequence
  1, 2, 5, 10, 20, ...

Extension Activities

1. In your pocket you have one dollar made up of 7 coins. What are the coins?
2. Fred has to give Mary's younger brother, Dave, 10 cents to get rid of him for a while. Fred feels cross about this, and every time gives Dave 10 cents in different coins.

    How many times will Fred be able to get rid of Dave? (Or, from Dave's point of view, how much money will he make if he keeps pestering Fred and Mary?)
3. Write a computer program to calculate the answer to:

'In how many ways can a dollar be changed into coins?'
4. Write a computer program to find the most efficient way of giving change for any amount less than a dollar.

    P.S. By 'efficient' we mean using the fewest number of coins possible.
5. If you only have 2 and 5 cent coins, what totals can you make?

Bag of Sticks

Introductory Activity

I have a bag of 12 sticks. They are all different lengths, each measuring a whole number of centimetres. I find that whenever I take three sticks out of the bag they will not make a triangle. How can this be possible?

What is the shortest possible length of the longest stick?

Extension Activities

1. Here are some interesting patterns in Fibonacci numbers. Can you explain why they happen?

(a) Here are three consecutive Fibonacci numbers:

$$2, 3, 5$$

Note that
$$2 \times 5 - 3^2 = 1$$
Investigate this for other sets of three Fibonacci numbers.

(b) Here are four consecutive Fibonacci numbers:

$$3, 5, 8, 13$$

Check that
$$5 \times 8 - 3 \times 13 = 1$$
Investigate this for other sets of four Fibonacci numbers.

(c) What do you notice about the sum of the squares of two consecutive Fibonacci numbers?

(d) Start with a unit square

Add another unit square

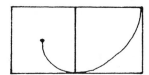

Now add a 2 unit square

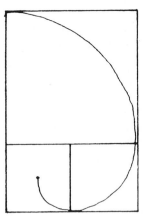

Continue to grow the spiral and use your pictures to find out about this sequence:

$$1^2 + 1^2 = 1 \times 2$$
$$1^2 + 1^2 + 2^2 = 2 \times 3$$
$$1^2 + 1^2 + 2^2 + 3^2 = 3 \times 5$$

(e) Work out these sums and continue them.

$$2^3 + 3^3 - 1^3 =$$
$$3^3 + 5^3 - 2^3 =$$
$$5^3 + 8^3 - 3^3 =$$

Bargain Offer

Introductory Activity

Commercial sugar cubes (the sort you get in a café) are smaller than the ones you can buy in a shop.

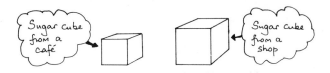

In fact, the commercial sugar cubes are about 2/3 the dimensions of shop-bought cubes.

If you usually take 2 lumps at home, how many would you expect to need in a café?

Extension Activities

1.

This looked like a bargain, but then I noticed that the 9 cent oranges were rather smaller

(6 cm diameter) compared with the 16 cent oranges (7.5 cm diameter). Were the small ones such a good buy?

Can you work out a rule of thumb for spotting a bargain?

2. There are many situations in which you do not use all of a purchase. For instance:

   • peeling a potato

   • a leg of lamb (you don't eat the bone)

   • the core of an apple

   • the stone of a peach

   • the wrapping on a sweet etc.

   In some cases the wastage is minimal; but in others it is quite substantial. Investigate!

3. For some purchases, the packaging makes the item seem much larger than it really is. As an example, we recently bought a large box that had a disappointingly small chocolate cake inside.

   Find ways of alerting your friends to the worst examples of packaging small items in large containers.

Best Magazine

Introductory Activity

If you could afford to buy only one comic or magazine a week which would be the best value for money?

Extension Activities

1. Draw up a plan of the perfect magazine.
2. Find out if others share your group's idea of a perfect magazine.
3. Make a list of recommendations that your group thinks would improve magazines.
4. Design a school magazine.

Board Games

Introductory Activity

Survey different types of games and their popularity.

Extension Activities

1. Design a board game with pegs (or pieces).

   Think about:
   • What different layouts are possible?
   • What alternative strategies are there (e.g. capture, following on, making a path)?

2. Design a game with cards or dice.

   Think about:
   • The role of chance.
   • What alternative styles are there (e.g. story-making, word guessing, collecting things of the same kind)?
   • How could your game be manufactured for sale at school ... to raise money for something?

   Think about:
   • costing,
   • presentation and marketing,
   • organisation of materials and labour.

Boys' Own Journal

These problems are chosen from the Boys' Journal of a hundred years ago. Are they too easy for us today?

1. How can 125 be divided in four parts in such a way that if you ADD 4 to the first part, SUBTRACT 4 from the second part, MULTIPLY the third part by 4 and DIVIDE the fourth part by 4, the answers are all equal.
2. There are three numbers whose product is 80. The first is more than the second by the same amount as the second is more than the third AND the sum of the first and third is twice the second. What are the numbers?
3. What number, when squared, will produce the digits

   1, 2, 3, 4, 5, 6, 7, 8 and 9?

(Today we can write a computer program for this. Try it!)

Calendars

Introductory Activities

Here is a month calendar.

S	M	T	W	T	F	S
			1	2	3	4
5	6	7	8	9	10	11
12	13	14	15	16	17	18
19	20	21	22	23	24	25
26	27	28	29	30	31	

(a) What do you notice about the number in each column and in diagonals (5, 13, 21 and 29)?

(b) Put a box round any four numbers, for example:

13	14
20	21

Find relationships between the numbers.
Have you tried adding pairs? Work out 13×21 and 14×20, then subtract. What's the answer? Try it for another box. Can you explain the results?

Extension Activities

1. Put a box round any nine numbers

8	9	10
15	16	17
22	23	24

Again, find relationships between the numbers. For example, find pairs of numbers in the box that add to the same.

2. Add up all the numbers (with a calculator) and divide the result by 9. Where in the box is the answer? Does this always work?

3. Do all these results work with any page of a month calendar?

Consecutive Numbers

Introductory Activity

Add two or more consecutive numbers from 1 to 9. For example, add

$$3 + 4 + 5$$

How many different numbers can you make?

Extension Activities

1. Some numbers can be expressed in several different ways as the sum of consecutive numbers. For example:

$$9 = 2 + 3 + 4 = 4 + 5$$
$$15 = 4 + 5 + 6 = 1 + 2 + 3 + 4 + 5$$

   What numbers can be expressed as the sum of consecutive integers and in how many ways?
2. What is the smallest number with 7 different factors?

Countdown

Introductory Activity — A game for 2 players
Rules

1. You need a pile of 15 counters.
2. Players take it in turns to remove 1, 2 or 3 counters from the pile.
3. The player who takes the last counter is the loser.

See if you can find a way of making sure that you win every time you go first.

Extension Activities

1. Change the rules so that the player who takes the last counter is the winner.
2. Choose any number of counters to make your pile. Also, choose how many counters can be taken away each time. See if you can still find a way of always winning when you go first.
3. Investigate the winning and losing positions in a Countdown game where the pile contains any number of counters and where players may only remove 2 or 5 counters at a time. (You can change the numbers 2 or 5 if you like.)
4. So far in the Countdown games you are allowed to use a number more than once as you count down to 1. Here's a new version of Countdown that has a twist in it. Each player has a number bank and each time the player uses a number in the bank that number cannot be used again (see the diagram which follows).

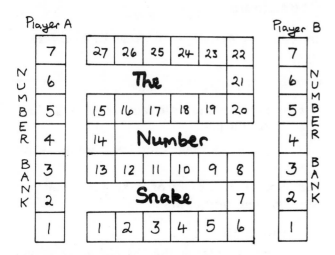

The Number Snake

Rules

Player 1 picks a number on the snake and covers it with a red counter. Then the players take it in turn to cover a number in their own number bank and move the red counter that number of squares down the snake.

The first player to count down to 1 is the winner.

Any player who has to count down below 1 is an automatic loser.

Cut it Out

Introductory Activity

Cut out a square. Draw two straight lines anywhere across the square and cut along the lines.

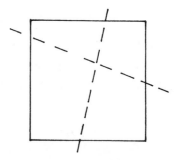

What shapes have you made?

Find what different shapes you can make by drawing the lines in different positions in the square.

Extension Activities

1. Try this with some other starting shapes. List all the new shapes that you think you can make, and check by doing it.
2. If you use more than 2 cuts, what new shapes can you make?
3. Write a computer program to demonstrate your findings.
4. Let's go on to solid shapes.

   An easy way of drawing a cube is to draw a square with another one behind it.

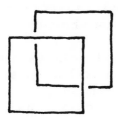

The next step is to join up the corners.

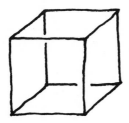

Let's see what happens if we cut this cube into two pieces with one slice. Here are some examples:

See if you can find out what shapes the slices make when the cuts are made in different positions.

5. If you have a good workshop at your school, you could make examples of some of the shapes you found in part 4. Also you could try making one of these famous puzzles:

These grooves are cut along the diagonal

Cut a regular tetrahedron into 2 equal pieces

Cutting up Shapes

Introductory Activity

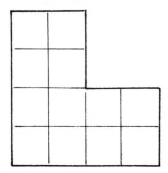

Show how this L-shape can be cut up into small L-shapes, like this:

Extension Activities

1.

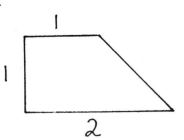

Show how this shape can be cut up into 4 pieces that each have the same shape as the original.
2. Find some other shapes that can be cut into pieces, each piece having the same shape as the original. One starting point is to look at regular shapes; also look for shapes that tessellate.

Dancing Marathon

Introductory Activity

Are you fit enough to take part in a Dancing Marathon? One way of finding out how fit you are is to take your pulse after resting. Then you should do about 10 minutes of vigorous exercise and take your pulse again. Five minutes later, after resting, take your pulse for a third time.

Discuss how fit you think you are when you have done all this.

Essential Information
How to take your pulse:
Place the tips of your first two fingers (not thumb) on the neck just under the chin, or wherever you can most easily find your pulse. Count the beats for 15 seconds and multiply by 4 (why?).

Resting Pulse Rate
The first time you take your pulse you get a rough idea of how healthy you are from this chart.

Beats per Minute	Fitness Gauge
Under 60	Very fit
60-70	Fit
70-80	Average
80-90	Below average
Over 90	Unfit

Recovery
Immediately after vigorous exercise your pulse rate will be higher, but if you are very fit, your pulse rate should drop back to the resting rate very quickly. The difference between the first and second measures of pulse rate is another indicator of how fit you are.

Extension Activities

1. How fit is the whole class?
2. Devise an exercise schedule and record your fitness and see how it improves.
   Any fitness project could involve:
   • substantial reading around the subject;
   • surveys of different age groups;
   • exploration of hypotheses such as 'swimming is more strenuous than running';
   • liaison with P.E. departments to devise training schedules.

Date Cubes

Introductory Activity

Using two cubes and numbers 0–9, can you label the cubes so that, by rearranging them, each date from 1st to 31st can be shown. For example, here the date is showing as the 29th.

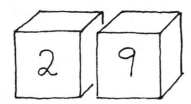

Extension Activities

1. How many cubes would you need to make up any complete date, and how would they be labelled?

   e.g. 25.12.85

2. Write a computer program that produces a calendar for next year, or any chosen year.

Digits 1 to 9

These activities have one thing in common; each involves the digits 1 to 9. For some of the simpler activities, it helps if the children have a set of nine counters with the digits 1 to 9 written on them.

1. Make a cross in which the sum across = sum down. For example:

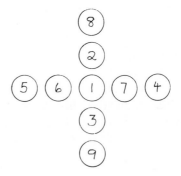

   In how many ways can you do this?

2.

   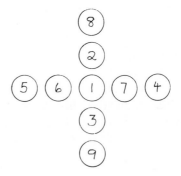

   All the digits - all the signs

Fit your nine counters on this diagram so that all the sums are correct.

3. A game for two players.

The digits 1–9 are put in a pool and the players take it in turn to pick a number. The object of the game is to be the first person to have three numbers that add to 15.

Hint to the teacher: Try using a pool of numbers set out in a magic square, e.g.

```
6 7 2
1 5 9
8 3 4
```

4.

Number A = (1)(9)(2)

Number B = (3)(8)(4)

Number C = (5)(7)(6)

Number B = 2 × Number A
Number C = 3 × Number A

Find another way of arranging the digits so that these equations are still true. How many ways are there?

5. Another game for two players.

Divide the digits into two sets, odds and evens. The first player has the odds set, the second has the evens set.

The game is to place the digits on a noughts and crosses board, and the winner is the first player to make a column or diagonal add to 15.

First Player
1 3 5
7 9

Second Player
2 4
6 8

6. Put the digits 1–9 in the boxes.

□ □ □ □ □
× .□ □ □ □

Make the answer as large as possible.
Make the answer as small as possible.

The next three activities are hard, but make interesting problems to solve by computer.

7. <u>Pierrot's Puzzle.</u>

Place four of the digits 1–9 on this diagram

so that the answer has the same digits in it,

e.g. 15 × 93 = 1395

8. Arrange the nine digits so that they form two numbers which, when divided, produce a given number, e.g.

$$13458 \div 6729 = 2$$

Make the results = 3, 4, ..., 9

9. Use the digits 1–9 to make

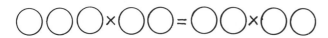

What do you notice about the answer?

Find the other ways of arranging the counters to get an equation that is correct.

Eureka!

Here are a few Eureka problems for you to try with the class. Eureka rules are:

1. The teacher can only answer a question from the pupils with 'yes', 'no' or 'irrelevant'.

2. When pupils think they have an answer, they must not call it out but shout 'Eureka!' instead. (Here's a practice go — 1 and 1 makes?)

3. After shouting 'Eureka' pupils should think of leading questions that give the rest of the class a hint.

4. Rules 1–3 must be strictly adhered to.

The solutions are necessary for these problems so we have provided them on page 125.

1. How many crosses are there on this piece of paper?

2. You have seven sweets. Then you eat all but four of them. How many have you got left?

3. Add six to itself six times. What do you get?

4. How many animals of each kind did Moses take on board his ark?

5. A plane crashed exactly on the border between New South Wales and Queensland. Where did they bury the survivors?

6. How far into a forest can a hunter and his dog go?

7. A man has but one match; he enters his apartment in the dead of winter and wants to warm it up quickly. He has a gas cooker, a paraffin stove and a woodburning stove. What should he light first?

8. A man enters a field with a package. He dies ... why?

9. A cowboy walks into a bar, points his gun at the barman, fires and misses. The barman gives him a drink on the house. Why?

10. Is it legal in Australia for a man to marry the sister of his widow?

11. A man drives up a hill at 15 km/h. How fast does he have to drive down the other side to make his average speed 30 km/h.

12. I have a coin in my hand. Think of a number. Add 1. Double it. Take away the number you first thought of. Do the last step again. Divide by four. What do you get?

13. A man goes bear hunting. He walks 1 km North, 1 km East and 1 km South and ends up at the same spot. What is the colour of the bear?

14. This is a story about John and Mary. John left the house one morning and slammed the door. A short while later Mary died. Why?

15. Two men walk into a bar and order identical drinks. One drinks very quickly and the other one slowly. One of them drops down dead. Why?

16. A man gets out of bed and goes to the phone. He rings someone up and says, 'Is Jones there?' The answer is 'No'. He gets back into bed and goes to sleep. Why?

17. I start with a glass of whisky and a glass of water, equal amounts in each. A spoonful of whisky is put in the water and thoroughly stirred. A spoonful of mixture is then returned to the whisky glass. Does the whisky contain more water than the water does whisky ... or vice versa?

18. Explain how this is made:

(Don't allow people to touch it, just look).

105

19.

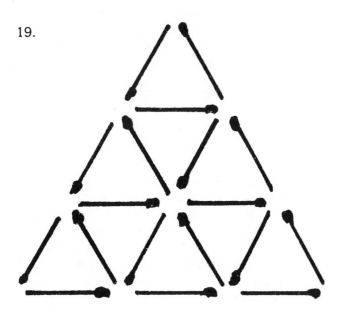

Remove 6 matches to leave 3 triangles.

Finger Exercise

These activities are designed to exercise fingers on the keys of a calculator.

1. Find a way of putting the digits 1–6 in these boxes so that the sum is correct.

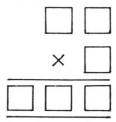

2. Is it always true that a larger number divided by a smaller number is greater than the smaller number divided by the larger number?

3. Take any two numbers that add to 1. Square the larger and add the smaller, then square the smaller and add the larger.

   (a) Guess which result will be the greater.

   (b) Try to convince a friend that you are right.

4. Find the largest product you can of numbers that add up to 17. Here are two to get you going.

$$8 + 9 = 17 \quad \text{and} \quad 8 \times 9 = 72$$
$$6 + 5 + 6 = 17 \quad \text{and} \quad 6 \times 5 \times 6 = 180$$
   (Going up!)

5. Try question 4 again, but with a number other than 17.

6. (Hard) For any two numbers, a and b, investigate which is the larger, a^b or b^a.

Fire Drill

Introductory Activity

How quickly could your class leave the school if the fire bell went?

- What is the route out of the classroom?

- How far is it?

- How long does it take to get out of school if you go sensibly?

Extension Activities

1. Is that the best route out of the school? If not, what is? Explain your findings to convince the rest of the class.
2. Repeat this activity for other classrooms that you use. Perhaps you could revise the school fire drill procedures.

In the Stars

Introductory Activity

Is there any similarity between horoscopes?

Look through the horoscopes from several of yesterday's daily papers and see what you come up with.

Extension Activities

1. Which daily paper's horoscope predictions are the most accurate?
2. It is claimed that the star you are born under determines your personality. Fact or fiction?
3. How reliable is a horoscope over a longer period?
4. This work could be extended to incorporate graphology.

I've Got a Rule

Class Activity

The basic idea of 'I've Got a Rule' is that children guess numbers that conform to the rule that the teacher has in mind. The activity starts by the teacher putting up 2 or 3 numbers that match the rule. For example:

Belongs   5 21 57   *all odd numbers*

Doesn't belong

The children then call out their guesses and a correct guess is added to this row; incorrect guesses are put underneath, as follows:

Belongs   5 21 57 3   7 ... and so on

Doesn't belong   72   8   12
                             6   14

When children feel confident that they know the rule, they should shout 'Eureka'. They can then continue to play, adding numbers that are aimed at helping others to see the rule, in this way testing that they really have got the right idea.

Examples of Rules

1. Odd numbers, even numbers, numbers with a particular factor.

2. Primes, squares, triangular numbers, Fibonacci numbers.

3. Numbers whose digits sum to 8 ('I 'ate this one!')

4. More than previous number, less than previous number. Two more than previous number, etc. The 'previous number' should always be the last one called out.

5. Any simple function of the previous number. Any rules based on the mathematics from your own maths syllabus are fun to use. Look for properties of numbers, or named sets that the children should have met.

6. There is no numerical pattern this time; the numbers are written on the board to form a diagonal shape. For instance, suppose the first 8 numbers to be called are 1, 2, 3, 4, 5, 6, 7 and 8. They are written on the board as:

Belongs   1 2 4 7 11

Doesn't belong   3 5 8 12
                       6 9 etc
                          10

7. You can also have fun with:

(divide each figure in half).

O, T, T, F, F, S, E,... (**One, Two, Three** ...)

Joining Triangles

Introductory Activity

Using 5 triangles shaped like this:

how many different shapes can you make?
Here is one to get you started:

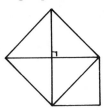

Extension Activities

1. This large triangle

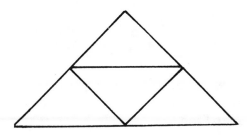

has the same shape as the original triangle.

Continue making even larger triangles. Write down how many small triangles each new large one takes. Can you find a pattern?

From this pattern predict how many small triangles will be needed to make the next triangle, and then the 37th.

2. What happens when you try to make this shape larger?

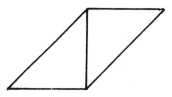

3. Choose other shapes of your own and see what happens when you make them larger.

Kick the Bucket

Introductory Activity

Using a 5 litre bucket and a 2 litre bucket, it is possible to measure 1, 2, 3, 4, 5, 6 and 7 litres of water. Show how each of these could be measured.

Extension Activities

1. Extend the introductory activity by using pairs of buckets of other capacities.

   Watch out! Some pairs of buckets will never enable you to measure 1 litre.

   Which pairs of buckets will enable you to measure 1 litre and which will not?

2. Large container problem

   A large container can only be filled using a 3 litre and a 5 litre bucket. What different quantities of water can be poured into the large container.

   Example: You can pour in 11 litres by pouring in 5 litres and 2 lots of 3 litres.

3. Extend the 'Large container problem' by using a variety of pairs of buckets.

4. Can you find a pattern in the 'Large container problem'?

Leap Frog

Introductory Activity

In the game of Leap Frog the aim is to swap the positions of two sets of counters. This is the starting position:

and this is the finishing position.

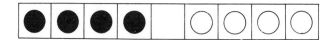

The counters can be moved either by sliding one place into an empty position, or by jumping over another counter (of the same or the other set) into the empty place.

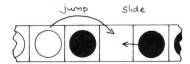

The white counters can only move to the right and the black counters can only move to the left.

Play Leap Frog.

Extension Activities

1. What is the number of moves you need to make to play a game of Leap Frog with 4 counters of each colour?
2. Find a way of explaining how many moves are needed to play a game of Leap Frog with 10 counters of each colour.
3. (Hard). Find out what happens when the rules change so that each jump is made over two counters rather than one.

We call this game 'Two-Leap Frog'.

4. (Harder). Find a way of explaining how many moves are needed to play a game of Two-Leap Frog with 10 counters of each colour.
5. For a change, try Three-Leap Frog, Four-Leap Frog, etc.

Lines and Dots

Introductory Activity

Put four dots on a piece of paper then draw all the lines joining two dots. What is the largest number of lines you can get?

Show how to get fewer lines by choosing special positions for the dots. Now try with three dots, five dots, and so on.

Extension Activities

1. Draw four lines on a piece of paper and mark a dot at each of the crossings. What is the largest number of dots you can get? Show how to get fewer dots by choosing special positions for the lines.
2. Find a rule for linking the lines and dots in both cases.
3. How many regions do you get with four lines, three lines, . . .? Again, can you find a rule?

MacMahon's Triangles

Introductory Activity

How many different ways can you find of colouring these three triangles using only 2 colours?

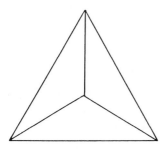

Extension Activities

1. What happens when you use 3 colours?
2. What happens with 4 or more colours?
3. Can you write a formula showing what happens for *n* colours?
4. What happens when you use a square, pentagon, etc.?

Magic N-grams

Introductory Activity

Find out how to place the numbers 1, 2, 3, 4, 5, 6, 7, 8, 9 on this triangle so that the sum of the numbers on each side is the same.

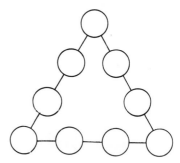

If this is too hard, encourage the children to 'try a simpler case' by using only numbers 1 to 6 on this triangle:

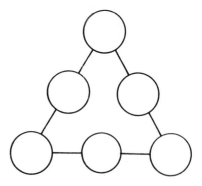

Extension Activities

1. Find out how to make this figure a magic 4-gram.

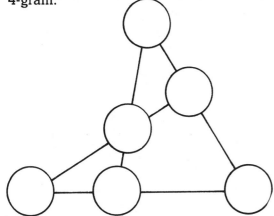

2. Find out how to place the numbers 1, 2, 3, 4, 5, 6, 8, 9, 10, 12 on the 5-gram so that the sum of the numbers on each side is the same.

3. Show how to put all the numbers 1 to 12 on the 6-gram so that the sum of the numbers on each side is the same.

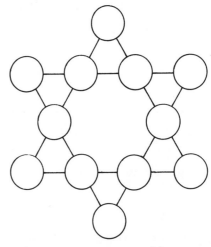

4. Continue with 7-grams and 8-grams.

5. (Hard). Did you notice that the numbers 7 and 11 are missed out for the 5-gram. Can you prove that the numbers 1 to 10 will not work for the pentagram?

Making Boxes

Introductory Activity

If you draw, cut out and fold this shape it will make a box.

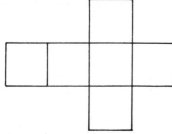

The drawing is called the net of a box. Find some other ways of making a net of a box.

Extension Activities

1. The good news . . . draw a snake that goes all around a box.

    The bad news . . . you must draw the snake before you fold up the box. How many different ways can this be done?
2. Design the net of a box that does not need glue or sticky tape to hold it together.
3. A spider is sitting at point A on a cube and a fly lands at point B (on the opposite face).

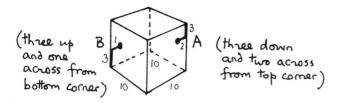

What is the shortest distance the spider has to crawl before it can catch the fly?

4. Suppose you have a sheet of cardboard and you want to use it to make a box without a lid. You can do this by cutting out squares at the corners and then folding up the sides.

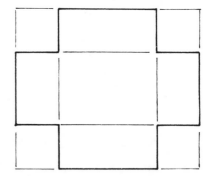

But suppose you wanted to make the box have the maximum possible volume. What size corners would you cut out if the sheet of cardboard is 15 × 20 cm? Try it for other sizes.

5. Design the net of a box that is not a cube, e.g. a Toblerone box. Can you make the snake go round this too?

Mini-Problems

Here is a list of mini-problem titles for you to use as starting points. Don't forget that an important feature of mini-problems is that the pupils should have to outline their own questions to ask.

1. Best buy notebooks/pencils/. . .
2. Design a space for living
3. Design a toy that four littlies could play with
4. Homework planning
5. Mobiles that rock
6. Newspaper sizes
7. Noughts and crosses
8. Our top twenty
9. Paper planes
10. Plan a healthy diet
11. Plan a housing estate
12. Pocket money

Mix and Match

Introductory Activity

Sam only likes fish fingers, spaghetti and chips. How many different meals can he have?

What happens if Sam suddenly finds he likes beefburgers as well?

How many different meals can you make up from your own favourite foods?

Extension Activities

1. If you wanted to look slightly different every day of the week, how many items of clothing would you need?
2. I found that I had 10 shirts, 2 pairs of jeans and 2 pullovers in my wardrobe. How many different sensible combinations have I got to choose from?

   I have enough money to buy 2 more items. What would you suggest I buy?
3. Using these ideas, plan your own wardrobe as sensibly as possible. Aim to cover all your needs, e.g.

   • school,

   • leisure,

   • sport,

   • smart occasions.

Paper Folding

Introductory Activity

Fold a piece of paper in half. Then make one more fold through the crease. Now cut in a straight line.

What shapes can you make in this way?

Extension Activities

1. Allow two or more folds through the first crease and, still using one straight cut, what shapes can you make now? Try to predict before you cut.
2. Which regular polygons can be made in this way?

Paving the Way

Introductory Activity

By joining 4 dots like this we get 1 slab with 4 outside edges.

By adding on another slab like this we get 2 slabs and 6 outside edges. As you see, we have not counted the enclosed (inside) edge.

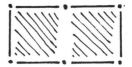

How many slabs make up this path?

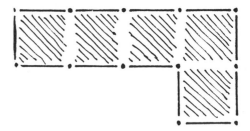

How many outside edges are there around this path?

Draw some paths of your own and see if you can find a pattern in the number of slabs and outside edges.

Extension Activities

1. This patio

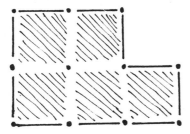

has 5 slabs, 10 outside edges, and 1 inside point.

Draw some patios of your own and see if you can find a pattern in the number of slabs, edges and inside points.

2. This patio has got a hole for a pond.

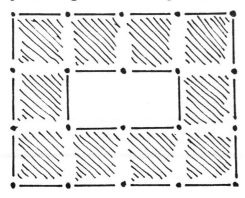

Find a new rule for patios with holes, as well as slabs, edges and inside points.

3. Investigate what happens when you use triangular slabs rather than square ones, e.g.

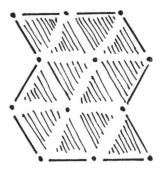

This shape has 10 edges, 12 slabs and 2 internal points.

4. Investigate what happens when the edges do not have to join points that are next to each other on the grid, e.g.

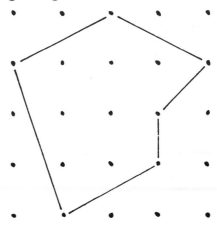

117

Real Problems

Here is a list of real problem titles that we have seen being worked on in classrooms. A title on its own says little about the potential scope of a real problem — that is for the children to define. We have grouped these into the three categories of real problem solving that we have observed.

Things to do:

• Reorganise the classroom to make it a better place to work in

• Improve wet playtimes

• School trip or holiday

• Sports day

• School Disco

• Setting up a tuck-shop

Things to make:

• The puppet theatre

• School garden

• Video/radio programme

• Youth Club

• Doll's house

Things to know more about:

• Taking good photographs

• How much pocket money you should have

• We get too much homework

• The litter problem

• Teachers do all the talking

Remainders

Introductory Activity

Find a number which, when divided by 3, leaves remainder 1, and when divided by 4 leaves remainder 2.

Find more numbers of this kind. Can you find a pattern?

Extension Activities

1. Try this again, but this time choose your own 2 divisors and your own 2 remainders.

   Some pairs of divisors and remainders won't work. For example, 3 and 6 don't work as divisors when the remainders are 1 and 2. Try them and see for yourself.

   Can you find a way of knowing in advance whether the divisors and remainders will work?

2. Find a number which, when divided by 3, leaves remainder 1, when divided by 4 leaves remainder 2 and when divided by 5 leaves remainder 3.

   Find more numbers of this kind. Can you find a pattern?

3. Try this again, but this time choose your own divisors and remainders. As before, can you predict in advance which sets of divisors and remainders won't work?

4. In medieval times, a very popular kind of puzzle was:

   A woman, when asked how many eggs she has in her basket, replies:

'Taken in groups of 11, 5 remain over, and taken in groups of 23, 3 remain over.'

What is the least number of eggs she could have in her basket?

Could you make up your own medieval puzzles?

Rolling Cubes

A cube is placed on the corner of a grid.

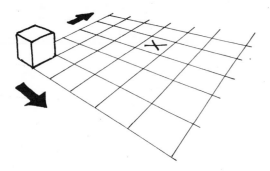

It can be rolled over an edge onto another square.

How many different ways are there of rolling the cube to the square marked with a cross?

(Rule: Moves can only be made in the direction of the arrows.)

Extension Activities

1. Find out how many ways the cube can be rolled to any square on the grid.
2. What happens with a triangular grid and a rolling icosahedron?

Room Temperature

Introductory Activity

How much does the temperature in the classroom vary at any one time?

Where is the warmest spot in the room?

Where is the coldest spot in the room?

Extension Activities

1. How much does the temperature in the classroom vary during the day.

   Is the warmest spot always the warmest spot?

   Is the coldest spot always the coldest spot?
2. Try this in the playground on a hot/cold/windy day.
3. How sensitive are people to changes in temperature?

   Are they any good at detecting the differences in temperature around the room without a thermometer?
4. How accurately can people tell the temperature? Set up an experiment to find out.

Spirolaterals

Introductory Activity

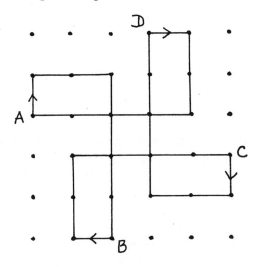

This spirolateral pattern is made by moving North, East, South and West by amounts 1, 2 and 4.

The first move is from A to B and goes
   North 1, East 2, South 4
The second move is from B to C and goes
   West 1, North 2, East 4
The third move is from C to D and goes
   South 1, West 2, North 4
And the last move is from D to A. It goes
   East 1, South 2, West 4

As you can see, the number sequence 1, 2, 4 is repeated in the directions North, East, South and West.

Draw the spirolateral for the number sequences

3, 5, 4 and 1, 2, 3

What differences can you find between them?

Extension Activities

1. Make up your own number sequences and see what spirolaterals they make.
2. In our examples we asked you to look at sequences of three numbers. Investigate what happens when you have more than three numbers in the sequence.
3. Write a computer program to draw spirolaterals.
4. Can you find a way of predicting the shape of a spirolateral when you know its number sequence?
5. Try drawing spirolaterals on triangulated paper. What happens then?
6. Can you make any general predictions about spirolaterals?

Statistical Starters

Here are a number of starting points that could be used as a basis for statistical activity.

1. All children enjoy football.
2. Boys are better than girls at general knowledge.
3. Ford makes the best cars.
4. You can never get the shoes you like in your size.
5. Nobody takes any notice of TV commercials.
6. They have yet to make a soft drink that we all like.
7. Boys get more of the action in children's books than girls do.
8. *Ghost Busters* was the best film ever.
9. The longer your legs, the faster you can run.
10. The lighter you are, the higher you can jump.

Surrounds

Introductory Activity

Arrange 4 tiles in a row.

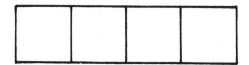

How many more tiles do you need to completely surround these 4? Make different shapes with the 4 tiles and find out how many tiles you will need to surround your new shapes.

Extension Activities

1. Try this using more than 4 tiles.
   Can you find a pattern in the number of tiles needed to make the surrounds?
2. What happens when you use triangular tiles?
3. Let's try this in 3D. How many cubes are needed to completely surround a single cube?
4. Can you find a pattern in the number of cubes needed to surround 2, 3, . . . cubes.

Three-Eighths

Introductory Activity

In how many different ways can you shade three-eighths of a 2 × 4 rectangle using whole squares. Here is one to get you started.

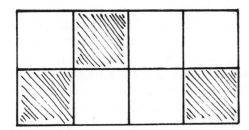

Extension Activities

1. In how many different ways can you shade five-eighths of a 2 × 4 rectangle using whole squares.
2. Make a chart of how many different ways you can shade one-eighth, two-eighths, three-eighths, and so on of a 2 × 4 rectangle. Can you explain the pattern?
3. Try this for other sizes of rectangle (and other fractions).

TV Ratings

Introductory Activity

What are the top 10 TV programmes with your class?

Extension Activities

1. Find out what the general public's favourite 10 programmes are. How does this compare with your class?
2. Which channel is the most popular?
   Why do you think this is so?
   Is it the same every week?
3. Use your findings to make recommendations for improving the popularity of a channel.

Weighing it Up

You can use only one each of these gram weights:

What's the heaviest object you can weigh?

What weights would you use to weigh an object of 6 grams, and one of 13 grams?

Show how to weigh any weight up to the heaviest.

Extension Activities

1. Show how you can weigh any object from 1 to 40 grams using only one each of these weights.

2. You can now use any number of 5 and 7 gram weights. Show how to weigh objects of 1 to 21 grams in weight.
3. Stamps

    Using only 5 cent and 7 cent stamps, what postage amounts can you stick on a letter?

Who Can Tell?

Introductory Activity

Can people really tell the difference between margarine and butter?

Devise an experiment to find out.

Extension Activities

1. There are lots of different manufacturers competing with different products; for example, you can buy different brands of coke, chips, baked beans and orange drinks. Who can really tell the difference?
2. One thing that does vary is the price that the manufacturers charge. Some people insist on paying more for their favourite brand. Are they getting value for money?

Solutions to the Eureka Problems
(from pages 104-6)

1. 2, there's a cross under the dollar.
2. 4
3. 12, each time.
4. Moses' ark was made of bullrushes.
5. Bury survivors?
6. Half way, after that they're coming out again.
7. The match.
8. The parachute didn't open.
9. The barman had hiccoughs.
10. A dead man can't marry.
11. He can't. $15 \div \frac{1}{2} = 30$ already.
12. Watch their faces if you show them a 1 cent coin sawn in half.
13. White
14. Mary was a goldfish.
15. The poison was in the ice.
16. The man in the room next door was snoring.
17. Same amounts of each in each. The water in the whisky came from the water glass; its place has now been taken by whisky.
18. Cut as follows:

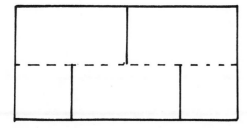

and twist the ends in opposite directions.

19.

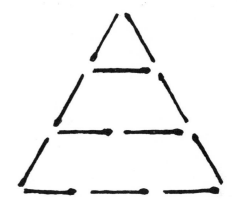

SELECTED BIBLIOGRAPHY

Barnes, D., Britton, J., and Rosen, H., *Language, the Learner and the School,* 4th ed., Heinemann-Boynton/Cook, Portsmouth, NH, 1990.

Bingham, A., *Improving Children's Facility in Problem Solving,* Columbia University Press, New York, 1958.

Bolt, B., *Mathematical Activities: A Resource Book for Teachers,* Cambridge University Press, Cambridge, 1982.

Brown, S.I. and Walter, M.I., *The Art of Problem Posing,* Franklin Institute Press, Philadelphia, 1983.

Burkhardt, H., *The Real World and Mathematics,* Birkhauser, Cambridge, Mass., 1981.

Gardner, M., *The AHA Experience,* W. H. Freeman, Oxford, 1977.

Lomon, E., *USMES: Guide to Guides,* Education Development Center, Newton, Mass., 1976.

Mason, J. H. with Burton, L. and Stacey, K., *Thinking Mathematically,* Addison and Wesley, Reading, Mass., 1982.

Mottershead, L.J., *Sources of Mathematical Discovery,* McGraw Hill, Sydney, 1979.

Mottershead, L.J., *Investigations in Mathematics,* McGraw Hill, Sydney, 1984.

Parnes, S.J. *Creative Behaviour Guidebook,* Charles Scribners' Sons, New York, 1967.

PME 233: *Mathematics Across the Curriculum,* Open University Press, Milton Keynes, 1980.

Polya, G., *How to Solve It,* Doubleday Anchor, New York, 1957.

INDEX